THE HORSE

THE HORSE LEADS THE WAY

HONORING THE TRUE ROLE OF THE HORSE IN EQUINE
FACILITATED PRACTICE

ANGELA DUNNING

YOUCAXTON PUBLICATIONS
OXFORD & SHREWSBURY

Disclaimer
The material in this book is intended for information and educational
purposes. It is not meant to take the place of either professional training or
diagnosis and treatment by a qualified medical practitioner or therapist. While
I offer suggestions and principles throughout for what I regard as good practice,
these are based on my particular approach to this work and with the specific
type of clients that I work with. If in any doubt, please seek professional advice
and training if necessary from an experienced practitioner or trainer before
incorporating anything I have suggested. No expressed or implied guarantee as
to the effects of the use of the recommendations can be given nor liability taken.

YouCaxton Publications
enquiries@youcaxton.co.uk

This book is dedicated to the horses who have saved me on more than one occasion and who offer humanity the chance of salvation and healing by reconnecting us to our hearts, our feelings and our bodies. I honor their guidance and unconditional love with these words and I write them for the benefit of both species.

FOREWORD

BY LINDA KOHANOV

Statues of Epona, the Celtic horse goddess, often portray her holding a cornucopia, a potent symbol of nourishment and abundance. Sometimes she's riding bareback, gently caressing a bridle-less mount who prances along *with a foal at her side*, emphasizing that it is a *mare* who carries this ancient feminine deity through the mists of time. Epona's horse is a mother in her own right, nourishing the next generation even as she assists her rider in reaching their lofty, wide-ranging goals.

In still other images, Epona sits on a modest throne. A herd of horses surrounds her... not bowing in submission, mind you. The earthy goddess appears to be hand-feeding her four-legged companions a pile of grain she holds in the folds of her voluminous skirts.

And then there's Pegasus, the magnificent flying horse of the Ancient Greeks. Most people know that the white, winged stallion helped heroes like Perseus kill the dreaded Medusa. But Pegasus too had a softer side. Lesser-known myths reveal that he was not only a stalwart companion to the Muses, he was a potent champion of creative awakening.

In one story, Pegasus flew up to Mount Helicon, the mountain of the Muses. There, he stomped his hoof firmly on the ground, creating a massive earthquake. In this act, the mythic horse opened a chasm in parched earth and solid stone, releasing a hidden spring. As the water gushed forth and cascaded down the mountain, it created an oasis of new growth. Forever thereafter, the river known as the Hippocrene (literally 'horse spring') flowed with inspiration. Artists, writers, composers, and inventors would hike into the wilderness to sit on its banks, drink its energizing waters, and listen to its gentle music, always returning with a new song, poem, painting, or vision of change and renewal.

Over the last 20 years, I've seen quite clearly that the myth of Pegasus lives on in our flesh and blood horses. When people are supported in spending time with these powerful yet nurturing animals, especially outside conventional training and showing contexts, horses reliably enact the Pegasus myth, opening deep chasms in our hearts, blasting through limiting habits of thought and behavior that have solidified through social conditioning.

At that moment, people suddenly have access to flowing sources of inspiration, intuition, and renewal that literally change their lives. Along the way, these same people experience the gentle ways of Epona, a goddess specifically associated with healing and transformation. Epona exercises her power, not as an ironclad warrior spurring her mount into battle, but as a strong feminine figure who forms a peaceful partnership of trust, nourishment, and mutual respect with her beloved horses.

The fields of equine facilitated mental health and experiential learning recognize that working with horses helps heal, empower and transform people in powerful ways that are nonetheless very hard to explain. Thousands of professionals worldwide now employ horses in the work of human development. But there are huge variables in the quality, approach and intention of these programs, some of which recommend treating the horse as a 'tool' rather than as a sentient being.

And then there are professionals like Angela Dunning, a practitioner who honors the horse as an intelligent, accomplished partner. Angela emphasizes that in order to help our mortal horses fully access their mythic healing abilities, we must take care of their social and emotional, as well as physical needs. In the process, we must approach them with compassion, gratitude, and a willingness to let them take the reins. Like Epona riding a bridle-less mare, one who can be trusted to set the agenda for a goddess associated with abundance and transformation, we too travel much farther in our equine facilitated practices when our horses are treated as professionals in their own right.

As Angela wisely advises, "We must be ever vigilant not to turn them into the tools of our trade once again, but uphold a reverence and respect for them and continually convey this to them through loving kindness and a gentle, wholly respectful working approach."

The Horse Leads the Way offers practical, soulful advice on exactly how to achieve this noble, yet wholly essential goal. Throughout her eloquently written book, Angela not only shows *why* equine facilitated learning practitioners and therapists must constantly do their own personal work, she outlines valuable tools and procedures for professional self-development. Along the way, she brings body, mind and spirit into play as she looks at a variety of facilitator training programs and natural horsemanship techniques popular in this field, with an appropriately critical eye on the benefits and the possible pitfalls of various approaches. Her focused, grounded view of what helps a *good facilitator* become an *excellent facilitator* is particularly inspiring. Most importantly, however, her good practice checklist for honoring the horse in equine facilitated therapy and experiential learning is long, long overdue.

Bravo Angela Dunning. With *The Horse Leads the* Way, you have accomplished what I hope that every person who graduates from the Eponaquest Apprenticeship Program will do: take the basic principles we teach, make them your own, bring your unique talents and expertise into play, learn even more from the horses themselves, and expand the field in your own right. Pegasus and Epona would be proud!

Linda Kohanov is the founder of Eponaquest Worldwide, and author of *The Tao of Equus, Riding Between the Worlds, Way of the Horse, The Power of the Herd,* and *The Five Roles of a Master Herder.*

PREFACE

This book comes into existence from carrying out more than a decade of Equine Facilitated Learning in partnership with horses to support peoples' growth. The purpose of my book is to put forward an approach to equine-partnered work which truly reflects the horses' wisdom. In this book I hope to make a powerful case for partnering with horses with integrity, honor and gratitude to our four-legged colleagues, without whom we cannot offer equine facilitated interventions.

I passionately believe that to be the most effective partner of a non-verbal, non-predatory mammal such as the horse, requires us to develop the following abilities and approaches: To fully trust our equine partners to bring forward their innate wisdom and guidance; to allow them freedom to express this wisdom unhindered; to be fully connected to our own body and its subtle sensations and messages; to be fully connected to our true emotional state; to be attuned energetically to all in our immediate environment, and finally, to be willing and brave enough to step into our own vulnerability and speak and act from our place of deep truth.

This requires a considerable commitment to our own personal development alongside our professional training. It has been my experience that the horses demand this of us and so it follows naturally for me, that to truly help our clients stretch beyond their current survival thresholds, we need to literally embody 'The Way of the Horse' in our professional practice and in the rest of our lives. Congruence is therefore essential in all that we do. Our mind-mouth-self must match up with our energy-body-self, otherwise our four-legged, highly sensitive somatic partners will feel our gap and we then cannot work in true harmony together.

Furthermore, as practitioners of an evolving inter-species partnership, we can do genuinely important work here by emulating these more advanced relationship approaches for our clients, many of whom are in need of help to readjust their own boundaries and heal from the scars of unhealthy or even abusive relationships. When the right conditions, lifestyle and way of partnering with our horses are in place, a harmony exists and the horses have limitless capacity to support, hold space and elicit healing in people.

This book will aim to engage practitioners, trainers and students of equine facilitated practice to consider how we can further enhance our work by fully trusting in our horses to bring forth the unique gifts they offer. My ultimate hope is to encourage all of us to deliver a valuable service in helping people, but which is in no sense detrimental to the horses we work alongside.

ACKNOWLEDGEMENTS

I would like to thank Linda Kohanov for lighting the fire of radical transformation, which burned so brightly in Arizona that I felt compelled to fly over the Atlantic six times to train with her, which changed my world forever and for Linda's generous, heartfelt words in her Foreword.

I also give my heartfelt gratitude to Kathleen Barry Ingram for teaching me and guiding me so expertly during my training at Epona and for her grounded, loving presence and support.

Sincere and heartfelt thanks to my good friend and fellow equine facilitated practitioner, Mike Delaney, for his enduring belief in me, for supporting me in recent times and his kind endorsement of this book. Huge thanks also to my dear Eponaquest® colleague Juli Lynch for her resounding endorsement of this book.

To my own beloved horses, North Star, Connie and LP, I remain eternally grateful for teaching me so much about myself, about horses, and their incredible potential to help humans grow and heal; without them this book would not be possible at all and I would not be the person I am today. I give them my heartfelt thanks and love for the depths they took me to personally and in enabling me to help others in their growth, as well as to understand the subtle intricacies of horse-human relationships.

Enduring gratitude and love goes to my dear Eponaquest® sisters, Kelly Ramey; Laura Amani Wilson; Helen Russell; Makanah Morriss; Susan Middleton; Jan Case Koerwitz; Ann Green Stern; Francine Phillips; Lisa Murrell and Georgie Stapleton, in whom I found true friends who held unwavering faith in me. Sincere gratitude goes to my trainers and mentors: Eve B. Lee; Kris Kramer; Shelley Rosenberg; Juli Lynch; Yvonne Monahan; Leigh Shambo and Mary-Louise Gould, for guiding and supporting me during our time together.

Finally, huge thanks go to my Editor, Valerie Ball, for all of her hard work and patience with me. Also many thanks to my friends and colleagues Victoria Standen and Cal Fowle for their invaluable help with proofreading, and in particular, sincere thanks to Fiona Hill for all her proofreading and support throughout this entire project.

CONTENTS

NOTES

For the purposes of this book, the general term 'equine facilitated practice' will be used to refer to all forms of this work, unless specifically stated otherwise. The acronyms EFL (Equine Facilitated Learning), EFP (Equine Facilitated Psychotherapy), and EFT (Equine Facilitated Therapy) will also occasionally be used when referring to specific areas of practice.

The term 'equine facilitated practice' incorporates all of the following: Equine Facilitated/Assisted Learning; Equine Facilitated/Assisted Therapy; Equine Facilitated/Assisted Psychotherapy; Equine Facilitated Human Development; Equine Facilitated/Assisted Coaching; Equine Guided Coaching/Learning/Therapy/Psychotherapy, but does not include any of the therapeutic riding models.

The suggestions I make throughout may not suit all clients and approaches, as this is a broad industry with an extensive range of clients and varying degrees of involvement of horses. I therefore recommend that you consider my offerings and then apply them accordingly to your approach and your clients' needs, should you choose to. I would also make the distinction that what I am suggesting is first and foremost for facilitators' own development to enhance their awareness and practice, and that by having these skills in your personal and professional toolkit, my hope is that you can engage with your horses and your clients even more effectively.

The views and approach put forward in this book are my own and while I am trained in the Eponaquest® Approach, they do not seek to represent the official Eponaquest® position, as inevitably, since graduating as an Eponaquest® Instructor ten years ago, the methodology being taught has continued to evolve. Therefore, there may be some differences in emphasis and approach between my suggestions and what is presently taught by Eponaquest®.

INTRODUCTION

There is something about the majestic arch of a horse's neck. The thundering power of a horse running wild and free with flared nostrils, alert eyes and pricked ears that makes us catch our breath. This exquisite animal has shared space with us both in the physical and mystical realms for thousands of years. As far back as our earliest ancestors, who portrayed hundreds of images of horses in their stunning cave paintings, the horse has captured the imagination and hearts of people.

These awe-inspiring, large, powerful animals continue to draw us towards them in new and fascinating ways. One of the most interesting in recent years has been the development of a movement employing horses to assist people heal from psychological and emotional struggles. This movement is known collectively as equine facilitated practice.

After more than a decade of working in this field, I am still astounded at the potential of what horses can achieve. The horses' wonderfully powerful insights and intuitions about what each person needs never ceases to amaze me and this is why this work keeps me constantly fascinated and fulfilled.

When allowed to, horses constantly offer us gentle guidance, reminding us to take better care of ourselves and each other. They bring wisdom that flows naturally from their finely tuned intuition and authentic way of being. They also remind us how to stay present and balanced, to conserve our energy for when we really need it, and to become more mindful, just as they are.

Closely connected to mind, body, soul and spirit, it seems horses can enable people to restore these same connections too. And it is in the area of the healing and development of the soul, that much maligned part of us in today's frenetic and mind-oriented society, that I find the horses can help the most.

Each horse brings something unique to this work. Each horse also brings something unique to each new client. And that same horse can bring something different to the same client on different occasions. Therefore, the potential lessons and healing are limitless.

While horses have been supporting people with physical and developmental disabilities for more than sixty years now, more recently they are also helping people heal emotional and psychological problems. These include debilitating relationship patterns such as codependency, poor boundaries and low self-esteem and confidence, as well as more complex conditions such as recovery from abuse, trauma and addiction. In addition, horses are now also being regularly employed to help managers and leaders develop a more authentic and compassionate style of leadership.

At the same time I have also witnessed equine facilitated practice flourish from a small group of pioneers to a truly global industry. This means that many more people can now experience the healing benefits of this unique work. However, this rapid expansion also brings a new set of challenges and I believe it is fair to say that our field of work now finds itself at something of a crossroads.

In many areas of this practice in the early days, the horses were clearly leading the way, guiding us through their lessons and feedback to help humans evolve beyond surviving to thriving and to help us reclaim our authentic selves. This approach was the antithesis of the traditional and long-standing *top-down* attitude that for centuries most humans have had to working with horses.

However, following the rapid growth of this field I believe that in some areas of practice we may have lost sight of what originally made this work so special. Most noticeable to me is that the more empowered and central role of the horses is at risk of being limited, as power has been taken back by the humans. In some situations it appears to me that the horses are employed as little more than 'tools' or as a means to an end for the client's benefit.

This innovative therapeutic partnership approach with another species also begs this fundamental question of us: Who am I to subject my horse to others' emotional and psychological traumas and needs? I would argue that, as the practitioners who form the human element of this inter-species partnership, we are the *guardians* of our equine partners. If we accept responsibility for this role as that of our horses' guardians, then I suggest that in exchange, we owe it to our horses to honor them throughout and be guided by them.

Unlike our human co-workers or business partners, our equine partners cannot exercise the ultimate form of choice by leaving the working relationship. They simply cannot open the pasture gate and head off for a new life. My belief, therefore, is that we need to be even more grateful and respectful of them in recognition of this limited position they are in, and one that for the most part, we have created.

So I believe the time is now right for a re-assessment of the role of the horse in this field of work.

Horses must not be peripheral to the process, but central to it. Their needs, suggestions, feedback and guidance are at the heart of this work. So it follows that their welfare, fulfillment and enjoyment must therefore also be central. Otherwise, we end up with little more than a continuation of more traditional uses of horses, where the needs of the horses are almost always secondary to the needs of the practitioners and/or clients.

Part One of this book explores what I believe makes up the essential components of delivering good quality equine facilitated practice. Central to this is the basic premise that if we respect and honor the horses as our partners, we will naturally create the best conditions for our clients to gain maximum benefit. In my view, the two are inextricably and intimately interconnected. Therefore, we will look at the true role of the horse; the central role of the horse's feedback and the importance of respecting the horse's boundaries. As well as the key skills a facilitator needs and the benefits of employing an embodied approach in our practice. I will also explore some of the other key areas of personal and professional development which enable us to practice effectively with horses.

I hope that this approach will appeal both to anyone already working in this field and to those considering training, who are looking for a subtle thread to weave into their own practice; one that gently binds you and your equine partners in harmony and which enables you to support your clients from a place of congruency and somatic presence.

I also attempt to place this work and the approach I recommend, in the wider context of the world we find ourselves in today. Facing environmental catastrophe, deepening inequality between rich and poor and abuse on a massive scale of the rights of women and children, the world is going through enormous shifts. Many believe this is a pivotal time: get it wrong now, and we and the planet are doomed. What the horses seem to be so clearly pointing us towards is a reconnection, yes back to our deepest selves, but also back to the natural world through their guidance.

At the same time, on a global scale 'The Feminine Principle', or 'The Divine Feminine' is finding her way back both into our individual psyches and into the collective. Again, for me, the horses' new role and offer to support us with making this reconnection, is a part of this return of feminine values, so aggressively suppressed and reviled for centuries. The horses are making the feeling life, compassion, empathy, the body, and love the corner stones of our way of being once again, rather than competition for resources, aggression and disrespect for life through a deep mind-body split. This is the focus for Chapter 3.

In Part Two some of the current industry wide issues will be explored further, such as training, regulation and terminology; the boundaries between Equine Facilitated Learning, Equine Facilitated Psychotherapy and Equine Facilitated Therapy, and the incorporation of differing horsemanship approaches in equine facilitated practice. I conclude with a general look at caring for our horses and other practical considerations in delivering our equine-partnered services.

I feel that part of the present dilemma that this industry faces is that, as horses are involved, equine facilitated practice is often mistakenly perceived as being closer to equestrianism (or horsemanship) than therapeutic or educational interventions. When in fact, due to the depth that horses can reveal to us about ourselves, this method is closer to therapeutic learning and psychotherapy. The problem that currently exists is that the former view is steering the direction of practice in some areas, whereas in my experience, the latter is usually much closer to the truth. This results in a number of issues concerning quality, ethical practice, and most importantly in the context of this book, how the horses are being treated.

A key problem with this perceived close relationship or cross-over is that many forms of horsemanship or equestrianism involve dominance-based approaches, which I feel can be anti-therapeutic for clients as well as not always being in the horse's best interests. As I will also aim to show, the horses seem to be offering us very clearly an alternative way of operating, and much horsemanship, including natural horsemanship, in my view, is still based on outdated attitudes and methods.

In writing this book, therefore, I am choosing to stand by the horses. My deeply held belief is that by embodying the ways of our equine friends, we can literally change ourselves and our relationships with them. In so doing, we are helping our clients and ultimately, our society, to become a more caring, feeling-based one that looks after all of its herd members. It is a privilege and honor to have embarked upon this path alongside these magnificent animals. I hope you will find some inspiration here for your own journey with horses helping humans.

Part I

THE HORSE AS A VALUED PARTNER

Horses have been supporting people for thousands of years and have been a primary vehicle for our evolution and development. They have provided us with means of transport, ploughed our fields, valiantly carried us into battle, and more recently, many people enjoy riding and competing horses each day both for leisure and sport.

During the 20th Century, people began to recognize for the first time that, in addition to the enjoyment of riding and caring for horses, there were also therapeutic benefits to be gained from being around horses. In fact, the physical, emotional and psychological therapeutic benefits of riding and being around horses can be traced back to as early as the First World War.[1]

Therapeutic riding began as a formalized practice in the 1950s in Europe and about a decade later in the United States. However, it wasn't until the early 1990s that what we now know as equine facilitated practice started to develop in its present form. During this period in America several therapeutic riding instructors, therapists and open-minded horse professionals began to notice the very real therapeutic benefits, in addition to riding, of spending time with horses. They began to incorporate sessions with horses into their therapeutic practices and educational programs, thus formalizing the field of equine facilitated practice. These people included, among others, Barbara Rector, Linda Kohanov and Kathleen Barry Ingram.

There are many reasons why horses are such powerful teachers and why this method can be more effective than traditional learning and therapeutic interventions for many people. One of the key reasons for me, is that horses are highly sensitive, intuitive beings which makes them extremely receptive *and* responsive to the body language, emotion, *energy* and *intention* of everyone around them. Horses also seem to have the ability to sense at a deeper, or sub-conscious level, what a person *needs* and what their vulnerabilities are in each moment. When that person is then open to a suggestion from the horse, a change in perception, behavior and emotion can take place in the person. It is because of this immediate, *direct access* to people's sub-consciousness that horses can often get to the crux of issues much more quickly than talk-based therapies, or other coaching and educational models.

From the 1990s onwards, a number of key organizations have emerged in this field, including EAGALA (Equine Assisted Growth and Learning Association), Epona (now called Eponaquest® Worldwide), EAHAE (European Association for Horse Assisted Education), and EFMHA (Equine Facilitated Mental Health Association) which is a sub-section of The Professional Association of Therapeutic Horsemanship International (PATH Intl.); previously called the North American Riding for the Handicapped Association (NARHA).

Since then the field has further expanded and we now have many more training and service providers around the world. This expansion is to be celebrated on the one hand, as it is offering an alternative form of effective intervention to many more vulnerable people with a wider range of issues. However, such expansion has also led to a number of key concerns including varying approaches towards the use of and role of the horses; an array of choice in provision for those seeking to access this method; confusion among those wishing to find suitable, good quality training; differing uses of methodology and terminology, and varying degrees of ethical practice.

In a prescient warning from 2005 *EFMHA* acknowledged that '*we are playing catch up to a field that has taken flight without a flight plan. If this field is to find a sustainable and a long-term mode of operation that will firmly lodge the methods into the realms of treatment and education, we must slow down and become educated about what we are doing.*[2]

However, most importantly for me, and which goes to the very heart of this book, is the wide variety of ways in which the horses are regarded and employed. In some areas of practice and training models, there is a real danger of the horse simply being an 'add-on' to the practitioner's methods, or a tool, solely there for the benefit of the client. This often also seems to involve a heavy emphasis on 'activities', involving completion of tasks, obstacle courses and games, with the horse playing little more than a means to an end for the client. This type of approach bears little resemblance to the subtle, deep and rich engagement that comes from being in relationship to horses in a calm, reflective space. Whereas, the horse's true role, in fact, is that of being the fundamental partner in the work, who is free to guide the process.

As we shall see, it requires much on the part of the human facilitator of this work to ensure we work harmoniously with our equine colleagues to gain the most benefit from working with them while also not burdening them in any way. I endeavor to explore as much of this side of the partnership as possible and in so doing, let the horses' wisdom flow out through these words.

In the second part of this book I explore in detail some of the industry wide issues which have developed over the past few years and which I have touched upon above. However, to begin with, I consider how I believe it is possible to deliver equine facilitated practice in a way which truly honors the horse.

Chapter 1

AN ETERNAL LOVE OF HORSES...

For as long as I can remember, horses have inhabited my life in one way or another, whether in my physical life or just nickering in my dreams or imagination; my love of horses is eternal. From a very young age I had an innate love of these animals and while we never had horses when we were growing up (my parents had enough of a task on their hands feeding and housing five children), I simply couldn't wait to be near them. I was a typical pony-mad girl and used to pray desperately for riding lessons, or a kind neighbor to take me riding with them and became ecstatic at even an image of a horse in a book or a movie. It seemed that I had somehow brought this enduring love and fascination for horses through with me at the soul level. There was simply no other explanation for it, or for my natural rapport with horses which served me well as I later twice embarked on a career involving horses.

Then one day, at the age of around eleven, my prayers were finally answered. A friend of my family had two ponies who needed looking after and riding and so I joined a long line of local girls who had also cared for and ridden them. For all of my teenage years until I left home for university, I was blessed to have full access to these ponies, spending every available second with them. They became my sanctuary away from my confusing home life and my mostly unhappy time at school. These two Welsh Mountain ponies literally saved my life during those stressful years. I would spend hours with them, grooming them, hanging out in the field or cleaning their tack; anything to bring me comfort and a sense of inner calm.

Of course, both of these ponies also became, without me realizing it, my earliest equine teachers. The smaller, grey one, called Beaut, was a very nervous, sensitive pony who, sadly, had also been through the experience of being caught and beaten by some local men. This left him terrified of men in particular, but also highly wary of all people. Somehow, though, I had the ability to reassure this scared little pony and I adored him, cuddling him much more than he probably wanted me to. The other, slightly bigger pony was a chestnut called Trigger. Trigger was a whole different matter. He was confident, sure of himself and ready to express his views at any moment. I was frequently terrified of him and we would often end up in a battle of wills, usually with him winning and me crying and heading back home deflated. He would act-up, refuse to move forward and buck or strike out at me if I was on the ground, squealing at me in anger.

Back then, I had no idea why he did this with me and yet would be as good as gold with other riders. Now, however, I fully understand what Trigger was trying to tell me: Be congruent and step into your power! I was forever trying to show some authority over him when I was literally quaking inside. I recognize now that because I had been powerless in my family and at school, my patterns of pretense and incongruence had become deeply ingrained. Yet Trigger could feel my power vacuum and my unwillingness to admit I was scared of him. His 'difficult' behaviors, I realize now, were an attempt to help me address my confused emotional states, yet my response then was to blame him.

These youthful experiences fueled my desire to embark on a career working with horses on leaving school. Nothing else really interested me and I suspect I gained such personal healing from being around them that I didn't want this to end. So at age sixteen I started working and training at a local riding school, helping care for and exercise the many horses and ponies that enabled this busy riding and training center to function. I also completed my initial riding instructor qualifications while there. However, this was to be a short-lived career as I was finding the business-like manner of running a riding school, in particular with regard to the role of the horses, difficult to accept. So, after working there for just over two years, I decided that a fresh start was the right thing to do.

I left my job at the riding school and went back to college to sit my 'A' Levels and then went on to university. Following graduation and in the intervening years between my first career with horses and when I picked back up some sixteen years later, I got involved in working in the not-for-profit sector. I began by supporting people with housing needs and then moved onto supporting refugees who had come to the UK following the Bosnian conflict. From there I went on to undertake community development with a wide range of marginalized groups in inner-city areas. This provided me with a diverse range of experience and also gave me ample opportunity to develop and hone my natural abilities to support vulnerable people.

During this time I was mostly unaware of my natural gifts such as empathy, sensitivity and intuition and equally why I found certain situations so challenging and stressful. It wasn't until my body gave way, due to chronic pain and accompanying depression and I was forced to stop working, that I began to turn my attention onto my own personal development. As I embarked on this new path, I discovered that I was one of the more highly sensitive people who make-up around twenty percent of the population and to my complete surprise and relief, that the challenges that come with this trait could also be turned into gifts. Further still, I was to discover, I could harness these natural abilities to the extent that I could even make a living from them.

It was at this point, when I was reading a book about being a 'highly sensitive person' that I came across a reference to another book called *The Tao of Equus* by Linda Kohanov. In the quoted passage, Kohanov was describing horses as being 'highly sensitive masters'. I immediately went out and bought *The Tao of Equus* and devoured it in just one sitting. It was like reading my own thoughts and feelings on each page. I resonated so deeply with much of what Kohanov was saying; I knew I had found my own personal elixir. This book quite literally changed my life and took me back into a world filled with horses once more, but this time in a radically different way. Here is where I also came across equine facilitated practice for the first time as I read about Kohanov and her team who were developing the Eponaquest® Approach (previously called Epona).

I was personally drawn to this emerging field of horses helping people as it brought together my passion for working with horses in a powerful and beautiful partnership, while supporting people's emotional, psychological and spiritual growth. It also fitted perfectly with my innate way of being with horses and my experiences of how immensely therapeutic they can be. I was particularly drawn to the Eponaquest® Approach for a number of reasons, most notably because the horses were regarded as sentient beings in their own right and it sought to allow the horse to be a teacher and guide. This approach also supports people to develop a working and spiritual *partnership* with horses in a highly innovative way, compared to all that has previously gone before in the history of human relationships with horses. But what Kohanov and her colleagues were doing which was so radically new, was bringing the elements and knowledge contained within these relationships into our consciousness, to intentionally help people develop their self-awareness and relationship skills.

So following what can only be described as a deep soul level calling, I travelled to the Eponaquest® International Study Center in Arizona six times over a two-year period to complete my personal development and professional training to become an Equine Facilitated Learning (EFL) practitioner. Not only did I receive excellent training, but on a personal level, for the first time in my life, I found a community that I felt I belonged to. For the first time ever, I was surrounded by people who held similar values about how animals were regarded; who did not label people as 'too sensitive' and who, like me, wanted to explore our special connection to horses. In addition and crucially in regard to this work, these were people who also sought to develop their own self-awareness and raise their level of consciousness. For the first time in my life I felt safe, held, loved unconditionally and supported by people who instantly 'got me', who saw my gifts and who wholeheartedly encouraged me to develop them. I had at last come home.

On returning to England at the end of my training, I eagerly threw myself fully into setting up and running my own full-time EFL practice. Strangely for me, this was initially back in my home town of Telford where I had grown up. Suddenly finding myself back there was a shock to begin with, but ultimately very healing. Now I was back as an empowered adult and about to embark on my dream career. So, from my old bedroom where I had survived my often painful teenage years, I started my dream EFL business.

After the first year I then moved out to South Shropshire, near the town of Bishops Castle in the beautiful Shropshire hills, an area of outstanding natural beauty and a part of the world I had always longed to live in. I had also by then acquired my very own herd of horses for the first time in my life. My dreams had finally come true and I was running my new EFL practice in partnership with my own beautiful herd, helping a wide range of clients benefit from this unique and powerful method.

Sadly though, after a few years of living this dream, life had other plans in store for me. Due in part to the worldwide economic downturn during that period, I experienced a range of practical and financial difficulties. These resulted in me having to relinquish my business in the form that it was then, including re-homing my three beloved horses. From then on, I continued to practice on a freelance basis working with a wide variety of horses in different settings until returning fully once more to my practice, a few years later. During this period I have also been fortunate enough to spend a great deal of time observing herds of horses in their natural habitats which has given me further profound insight into equine behavior and needs. More recently, I began networking and sharing practice with colleagues from all approaches of equine facilitated practice in the UK. This has offered me a valuable additional perspective on how some areas of this work have developed and, most particularly, how the horses are being involved outside of my own approach and that of Eponaquest®.

Chapter 2

My Approach to Equine Facilitated Practice

Allowing the horse's natural, intuitive instinct to flow at all times, is the key to this work.

One of the primary reasons I was drawn to Eponaquest® in particular was because of how they viewed the horses as sentient beings in their own right. They also firmly put the horse's role and well-being center stage. This is stated in their Best Practice Guidelines as thus:

'We regard the welfare of the horses entrusted to our care as paramount to the work of EFL. The horses' choice to engage in this work or with a particular client is honored, trusted, and supported at all times, as is their health and care. We are open to constructive feedback on their care and well-being.'[3]

The methods I encountered at Eponaquest® were profoundly guided by the horses' suggestions and feedback. This resonated deeply with me as I had left the traditional equestrian world some years ago, disillusioned with how secondary the horses' needs and voice was. The horses' wonderful gifts, well-being and the sense of them as sentient beings, was completely disregarded in that world. So, when I found a much more equal way of partnering with horses, I was overjoyed and relieved.

Since then, during my experience in this work, I have gradually adapted and refined my methods to develop what I consider to be my own, distinctive approach. I believe that the methods I use offer a subtle yet deep and effective approach to engaging with horses. Underpinning my whole approach is the concept of regarding the horse as an equal partner. I have found that by just employing some simple, mindful skills as facilitators, we can enable our horses to work more freely and therefore derive even more benefits for our clients. This empowers the horses to express who they are, shifts us away from the danger of the horse being used as a means to an end, or a tool, and opens up outcomes we may never have previously envisaged for our clients.

Much of my approach is based on the simple premise that when we are letting the horses do things that come naturally to them and which they are innately good at, then we will also obtain the best outcomes for our clients. This approach therefore places a large emphasis on such aspects as working with the body and emotions as well as the mind, respecting the horse's boundaries and regarding the horse as a sentient being in his own right. In later chapters I also cover specific additional skills such as being aware of the False Self and working with groups, as well as key areas of personal development for practitioners.

However, in the remainder of this chapter I mainly concentrate on two aspects of my approach which I believe are fundamental to honoring the role of the horse in this work: *Honoring the horse's feedback at all times* and *skilled facilitators as conduits for this work.*

Honoring the Horse's Feedback at all Times

Equine facilitated work first originated from a small number of perceptive people realizing that when they really paid attention, they could see that horses were giving *vast amounts* of feedback about people's emotional, psychological and physical states all of the time. I believe that this is potentially the central feature which makes equine facilitated practice such a highly impactful form of therapy and learning, and therefore I wish to encourage a renewed focus onto the horses' feedback.

Crucially, it is through allowing healthy and empowered horses to play the role of what I see as an honest and neutral mirror to a person, that we can gain valuable feedback from the horse as to what may be ready to come into the awareness of the client. This can be anything from the subtlest degree of change, such as a renewed focus on their breathing, to a full-blown cathartic release of pent-up emotions. The feedback from the unbiased mirroring of the horse is the central way that equine facilitated practice works. The primary role of the facilitator therefore, is to notice, respond to and when appropriate, sensitively reflect that feedback to the client.

Every single thing from the horse is potential feedback. The horse literally acts as a huge bio-feedback capability for us, energetically, emotionally, physically and spiritually. As the human part of this working partnership, a key part of our job is to notice the horse's feedback and move forward with our clients according to that feedback, not according to our needs or agenda. Inherent in our role, then, is to be the observer and sensor to what is taking place between horse and client.

Also inherent in our role is to be able to empathize with our horses as well as our clients. In any moment a horse may exhibit some discomfort or distress, or express a need. This may be solely to do with themselves, or any of the people around so the facilitator needs to be attuned empathetically to her horses and respond accordingly. Without empathy we cannot really sense what our horse may need. Empathizing then inevitably ensures that we look after their welfare in each moment and thus is an inherent ability in a working relationship with another sentient being.

Our job, once we start the session, is to watch what the horse does. From the moment the client is in the horse's vicinity, we need to be watching the horse for information. Sometimes this feedback is really clear and obvious, for example, if the horse has freedom of movement and choice and chooses to stay well away from the client, or if he comes closer to the client. Sometimes, though, the horse's feedback is very subtle; almost imperceptible and easy to disregard if we are not tuned in energetically and being *really* attentive. Either way, their feedback can be easily dismissed, if we are being too casual, or we deem it irrelevant, or interpret it as *just* equine behavior to do with themselves or their herd.

What the horses do physically gives us the most useful information, as they are incredibly physical, intuitive beings. This is in contrast to humans, who are predominantly cognitive and verbal beings with a tendency to cover up or ignore their involuntary physical body language and cues. Horses move and behave spontaneously from instinct and need, rather than premeditated thought or conflicted emotional states like we often do. Therefore *whatever* the horse does physically is significant. To have a full and firm grasp of this is essential to be able to do this work well. It can be so tempting in our enthusiasm to let our own input and skills take precedence over the much more subtle movements and feedback of the horses, but we do this to the severe detriment of our clients or trainees. Crucially, though, we also do a huge disservice to our horses. After all, why have the horses present if we don't fully attend to *their* feedback?

The next most important type of feedback is energetic feedback and so it is important for the facilitator to develop energy awareness. That is, awareness by the facilitators of the constantly shifting energy, which includes the continually fluctuating emotional and physical state of themselves, their clients and the horses. It is well known in this work that the horses feel and mirror the emotional energy and physical state of the people in their environment. Even equestrians with no interest in this type of work acknowledge that their horse will pick up on their mood. Therefore, staying attentive and tuned in to the behavior and energy of the horses enables the facilitators to sense what may be happening with the person or group of people.

I observe and energetically and somatically tune into, the

behavior and feedback of the horses as much as possible. From the moment the client enters the same space as the horses, the horses are in my peripheral vision or 'soft-focus'. In this work our task is to be attentive to both our client and the horses. This is why this work is not necessarily easy. We need to be able to fully attend to our client, whose well-being is our number one priority during a session, while simultaneously having our peripheral vision on the horses, to notice their responses to the client. If we sway one way more than the other too much, we risk missing something vital from the horses or we risk letting go of our client, who needs to feel fully supported all of the time. As our highly sensitive bio-feedback partners, this is the number one way to ascertain what might be happening for the clients. Whether working one-to-one with a single client and one horse, or with a group and a herd of horses, it is by watching the physical behavior of the horses that the information can be gathered to help our clients. As well as paying attention to the changes in the horses' energy.

If we just look at one example of the fundamental role that horses can play, which is that they are exquisitely sensitive to incongruence in people. Horses often mirror our true inner state, rather than relating solely to the mask or facade that we are trying to project to the world, which is what so frequently happens between people. When around incongruent people, the horse often moves away and seems disinterested. This is key fundamental feedback from the horse to the practitioner. As Arianna Strozzi comments in her book *Horse Sense for the Leader Within*:

'With this equine hypersensitivity to surrounding landscape, including inconsistent or incongruent behaviors in humans, the horse appears to 'mirror' human internal feeling through its observed behavior of distancing and non-interest. Horses have a highly curious nature, thus, behaving disinterestedly is remarkably unusual.'[4]

Disregarding Feedback; Why and How This Might Happen

When feedback from the horse is disregarded or denied, this could be because the facilitator does not feel they have the skills or confidence to deal with the client's difficulties. These 'difficulties' are most likely to be a block caused by some strong emotions which may be just about to surface, hence the feedback from the horse who feels this pressure building in the client. So the most effective approach with blocks is to work gently with the client to help facilitate the acknowledgement and release of these feelings. By watching the moment to moment feedback from the horse, you can more easily begin to sense where the client may be in their process, and use whatever tools you have in your facilitation toolkit to support them through this sometimes painful, yet potentially transformative experience.

However, it could also be that the facilitator does not perhaps understand the significance or symbolism of the horse's feedback. This is where substantial experiences of horses and rigorous training play a crucial role in preparing practitioners for this work, to ensure the horse's feedback is valued and thereby give our clients maximum opportunity for growth.

To illustrate, let me give a few examples of ways in which the horse's feedback could be missed or overlooked:

1. A horse shows an indication of working with a particular client, but another horse is chosen by the facilitator instead.
2. A horse shows an interest in a client, but then walks away; but the facilitator doesn't then follow through with the client to find out what they were thinking or feeling both when the horse was nearby and when they left. This is a missed window of opportunity to explore the horse's feedback.
3. When teaching how to move a horse around loose in a round pen or arena (active round pen work), if the horse

refuses to move for the client but will move for the facilitator, then it is most likely to be due to a block in the client. If this is with a group and again the horse moves for some participants but not others, then some people are clearly experiencing a block. If, however, the horse refuses to move at all for anyone, then perhaps they are not the right horse for that session on that day... they may have a health or mobility issue or are just not keen on this particular activity. A horse refusing to move looks the same, regardless of the reason behind it, but by carefully eliminating incongruence or lack of clear assertive intention in you or your clients, then you can be more certain of what your horse is communicating to you. Then you can either focus on the emotional state of the people involved, or correctly switch horses. In my many years of doing this particular activity, I have rarely if ever had to switch horses, but I have had to help my clients discover and move through a block in them on almost each occasion. My experience tells me it is almost always to do with the person and almost never to do with the horse. This example demonstrates the skill and the courage needed by the facilitator to help their client go beyond general 'technique' and instead, go within, and face some perhaps difficult feelings or self-beliefs. It is much easier to blame the horse and make life easier for your client and yourself, but that will deny this work justice. It also illustrates how a body-focused approach can be so helpful to explore the feeling state of our client. I will speak much more about the role of the body in Chapter 6.

4. A horse is approached by a large group of people, a common exercise in many leadership programs, and the horse's boundary cues are completely ignored by both the clients and facilitators. The people approach and go right into the

horse's immediate personal space and usually also touch and move the horse.

5. Very clear cues from a horse indicating that he does not wish to be touched, are ignored. The horse pins his ears as the person enters into his personal space, pinning them more tightly back as the person goes to touch and keeping them pinned. The horse also tries to move away from the touch.

Interpreting Feedback

When facilitating, the most effective way to discern whether the horse is telling you something about themselves and their needs, or whether they are reflecting back something about the client, is to ask the client to check-in with their body. Is there a block? Is there a strong feeling coming up? What are they thinking? Is their False Self telling them a negative message in that moment? The latter is, by the way, usually the main culprit. By getting the client to focus on themselves you can then see if the horse's behavior shifts in response. Usually it does and then the session can proceed. *If*, however, the horse maintains its behavior, for example, the horse goes and stands by the gate of the round pen, then this could well be that the horse is saying the interaction with the client is finished as far as they are concerned. Often, horses who have freedom of choice and movement when working, as opposed to being restricted through the use of a rope, will indicate when they feel the interaction is complete for the client. However, learning to discern this particular message from one where they are saying they are unhappy with working more generally, or wanting to go back to their herd or field, is important for facilitators of this work. Again, these are subtle differences and here is where we need to work with our own intuition and sense what the horse is indicating through their feedback in order to best meet their needs and those of our client.

It is possible, of course, to misinterpret the horse's feedback and especially when we may be nervous, experiencing performance anxiety, our inner critic or False Self is unconsciously activated, or we are out of our personal comfort zone as facilitator (see Chapter 8 for a more in-depth discussion on the False Self). When we are 'triggered' like this, our focus tends to be on how we look and sound, or how our reputation may be perceived. If this happens we are then at risk of losing the connection to both our own inner guidance system (our body, intuition, emotions and energy) and to our horses. As a result we can then misinterpret their feedback.

There are many fine lines involved in this work and we won't get things right all of the time, but this is where our own self-awareness, congruency and clear boundaries come into play. As does the confidence to gently, but effectively, support your client to return their focus over and over again to themselves, their body and their present state of mind. Learning when to spot a horse is saying 'I'm done' is vital to maintain your horse's well-being and enjoyment of their job with you. Of course, it again requires you to be humble enough to take the lead from your equine partner and thus step into a true inter-species partnership.

Understanding The Horse's Physiological Feedback: Licking, Chewing and Yawning

Having just looked in general terms at the importance of honoring the horse's feedback in all of our equine facilitated practice, I now want to focus in detail on one specific type of feedback, namely the physiological feedback; in particular, the horse's responses of licking, chewing and yawning.

In my experience, working with this type of feedback is a fundamental aspect of equine facilitated practice and is therefore at the heart of my own approach. It is, however, a complex subject and one which is currently open to interpretation and confusion both within this field and general equestrianism. It is also an emotive issue and one which is currently being debated in terms of whether, and to what extent, stress is experienced by horses in their interactions with humans, including in equine facilitated practice. What follows is my own understanding, based on many years of undertaking equine facilitated practice, of what the horses tend to do and why; plus some personal experience of horsemanship and equine healing.

As already described, honoring all of the horse's feedback is the primary way we are able to work in partnership with them. This is for two reasons: It directs us, as the facilitator, towards how our client may be feeling. Further, it is the only way we can really assess, in the moment, how the horse is feeling. Therefore, it is imperative that practitioners recognize and understand the feedback of the horses to both effectively deliver this work and to assess the horse's well-being throughout the session.

In this work our first aim must always be to create non-stressful situations for our horses at all times. We want the horses to act as a neutral mirror for our clients. If the horses are stressed themselves in any way they cannot do this and it contaminates or even invalidates the feedback they give us about our client. By ensuring, as far as possible, that the horses are not caused any stress, this enables us confidently to conclude that if the horse exhibits some physiological responses such as licking, chewing and/or yawning, it is because of an emotional and physiological release taking place in the client. If we blur this through either stressing the horses or ignoring their physiological feedback, this method simply doesn't work.

As discussed throughout this book there are several steps we can take to ensure that any stress for the horses is kept to a minimum. One of the most important is by ensuring that we do not create situations where incongruent people interact with horses, and especially in confined spaces or through the use of equipment in the form of halters and ropes. Incongruence presents in people in a range of ways, these are typically: stress, tension, disconnection from the body and emotions, being ungrounded, dissociation, and/or being primarily False Self driven. This is why carrying out some initial preparation such as the Body Scan, Meet the Herd, breathing exercises and boundary awareness must be undertaken before placing a horse and client in a restricted area (see Chapters 7, 4 and 5 for more details of these techniques). Freedom of movement and choice for our horses is another extremely important factor as it goes a long way to eliminating this risk of equine stress from the outset. It is also, of course, how we can further help our clients through noticing whether the horse chooses *not* to engage: by them not coming over or very near to the client, this gives us the feedback that the client may be presently incongruent. (See more on this in Chapter 4).

Once we have minimized the amount of stress felt by the horses, we will then be in a position to interpret the horse's feedback for our clients.

As already mentioned, some of the most frequent and important types of physiological feedback that we need to be aware of and understand in this work specifically are when the horse begins to lick, chew and/or yawn.

This type of response from the horses is often interpreted in several different ways. However, I also feel very strongly that it has been greatly misunderstood and confused in certain areas of equestrianism, for example, in natural horsemanship it has a very different meaning to how we interpret it in equine facilitated practice. Unfortunately, some of this confusion and misunderstanding has crept into this work too, inevitably perhaps, given the present overlapping of the two fields. Ideally, I would like to see these two fields become entirely separate as I feel there are some inherently detrimental effects to both horses and clients in using natural horsemanship approaches. In Chapter 14 I discuss my reasons for this in more depth

20

where I focus specifically on the use of horsemanship in equine facilitated practice.

Here, though, I will concentrate on how we need to be working with this equine feedback in our specialist practice and, due to its vital importance in this work, why I feel it is crucial to try and clarify this information from the horses and our understanding of it.

Different Interpretations

In natural horsemanship, the horse licking and chewing is commonly interpreted in two main ways. The first interpretation is that it is deemed to be a sign of the horse 'processing what they have just learned'. It is taught that it is the cue for the handler to release any pressure they are applying to the horse; for example, to stop asking the horse to move away from them.

It is also taught that it is the feedback to the handler that the horse has chosen to submit to them as their leader. This is seen when the horse begins to lower its head, seems to soften its body posture and then often begins to lick and chew. You see this in young horses and more submissive horses in herds, who communicate to the other horses that they accept their herd position. However, please see below regarding the following points: the inherent degree of stress I believe is involved in this act of submission; how I see this occurring within a lot of horsemanship and training, and why I feel it is so dangerous if this is included as a *goal* in equine facilitated practice.

I have always had difficulty accepting the first interpretation often given by many natural horsemanship proponents, as I don't believe horses cognitively 'process' learning in the same way that we do. It never seemed to fit for me and I always suspected it was simply a handy human explanation to justify a response from the horses that was not *quite* being fully understood... If the horses are processing in any way when they lick and chew, I strongly suspect it is because they are *emotionally* processing or integrating something, which does indeed fit with what I see in my EFL work and when I have experienced healing taking place in the horses themselves.

My difficulty with the second interpretation is that this understanding has been used as a desirable approach and goal in many areas of natural horsemanship. As a goal of horsemanship, and in terms of the impact on the horses, I am personally completely opposed to this. Further, I feel very strongly that such an outcome is counter-therapeutic and therefore is highly undesirable if incorporated into equine facilitated practice.

Why I Believe Horses Lick, Chew and Yawn

As already discussed, this is a complex and somewhat controversial subject. There seem to be a number of situations when horses lick and chew and the reasons for licking and chewing are still not yet fully understood. Many people believe that stress plays a major role and it is undoubtedly the case that licking and chewing in horses is sometimes a sign of stress. However, it is my own experience that horses also lick and chew when at complete rest, for example, when in their field, and therefore clearly not experiencing any stress at all. They also sometimes lick and chew immediately prior to drinking and eating. Further still, in my EFL experience, it is the case that horses will lick and chew when a person in their vicinity is beginning to *acknowledge a personal truth, release a state of tension in their body, or feel an emotion,* and the horse chooses to actively participate in the emotional release, in the form of support. In this situation the horses tend to *choose* to come closer to a person who is having an emotional release, almost as if they are helping the energy move through the person, and obviously would not do so if it caused them stress to any degree.

As I said, often the horse begins to lick and chew when a client begins to access or acknowledge a truth – a core feeling or belief about themselves. If the person then allows this feeling to emerge more fully and, particularly if this is then felt and expressed through the body and especially crying, the horse will in turn also release more fully, often through yawning and sometimes, urinating or defecating, as well as lying down or rolling, too. Male horses often also drop their penis.

What I believe is happening here is that the horse is feeling the release of tension in the person's body and energy field as their emotion moves up and out of them. In this moment, the person comes into congruency, or alignment of their emotions and awareness. The person may speak in more detail, begin to cry, their body may shudder or convulse, and they may bend over, sit down, or want to touch the horse for comfort and support. My understanding of what is happening in the client is that this is an emotional release, accompanied by a physiological release of, and change in, muscle tension, heart rate and breathing. All of this, until the emotion is released, feels exactly like tension, or stress in the person. Often, just before we access a true feeling, we feel tense and tight. Once our dam breaks, and especially if we cry, our body relaxes and the horse beside us also begins to relax, which is frequently displayed through licking, chewing and yawning.

In equine facilitated practice therefore, the horse beginning to lick and chew is a key indicator as it helps us know that our client is reaching a core issue or truth about themselves; that they are making a breakthrough and a deeper connection to themselves. We watch our horses and when they begin to lick and chew and/ or yawn, we sense that something significant is happening with our client.

In my experience, this is definitely not the horse 'submitting' to either us or the client, (and indeed, we surely would not desire this to be the case). Nor is it because the horse is himself stressed. This is instead the horse participating in, or facilitating the 'releasing' of the pent-up feeling, energy or tension taking place in the client. This often happens in this work when the person also moves from their False Self persona and into their True Self. (See Chapter 8 for a more in-depth discussion on the False Self).

To complicate matters further still, when horses yawn without licking and chewing first, this seems to also happen when horses are themselves having an emotional and physiological release. For example, I have often seen this happen when a horse is receiving some healing.

The Role of Stress

When a horse is put under pressure, for example when we ask her to move, this is stressful to her to varying degrees. When horses move each other around in a herd there is some stress involved. Their heart rate increases, their muscles tense, they may feel afraid or angry, depending on the situation and which horse is moving which. So, when a person emulates this and moves a horse around and the horse begins to lick and chew, the horse is actually releasing his _tension_ or stress in his body and emotional system. The fact that this happens simultaneously as the horse is submitting is where, I believe, the misinterpretation has arisen.

Stress is caused by a build-up of tension in the body. In horses, this is most likely connected to their emotion of fear, as this is one of their primary emotions that they are hard-wired to use to go through life safely. So, in fact, in many traditional and natural horsemanship approaches, what is actually happening is that the trainer is making the horse afraid of them. _They_ are causing them some degree of stress. So when the horse finally gives in, as any animal which is preyed upon in nature does when it knows it is in its immediate best interests and to avoid further stress, confusion or pain, they have to then release this stress from their body.

When under stress and in a confined space alone with a human with a rope or stick, unless the horse can jump out and escape (flight mode), or attack the human and disable them (fight mode), then all they are left with is to *submit* (freeze mode) in order to stop the pressure being applied. In other words, they give in or, as Ariana Strozzi describes; they choose to *appease*.[5] When the horse gives in to another, stronger, herd member, they then release their tension that has built-up. When the pressure is released or dropped, the horse can then begin to release its tension and so starts to lick and chew. What is greatly missing from the teachings and understandings in a lot of horsemanship is *why* the horse licks and chews – the cause of the stress and tension *beneath* the physical symptom of licking and chewing. This is casually skimmed over; ignored, in fact and only the *act not the cause* of submission is focused on, talked about, and worst still, is even taught as a goal to aim for with pupils of these methods.

To work in one field which interprets licking, chewing and yawning as one thing, and see another approach interpret it as a successful act of submission brought about through dominance, (even if they perhaps don't acknowledge it as such) is something that has concerned and perplexed me for years. This is also why, in my view, it is dangerous to have too much of a cross-over between equine facilitated practice and natural horsemanship. You can see with this fundamental issue with regard to the horse's response, that trainees and practitioners could be confused and potentially misinterpreting the horse's feedback, thus also potentially confusing clients about what is actually happening *and* causing stress to their horses unwittingly. Indeed, to misinterpret licking and chewing in equine facilitated practice could be hugely detrimental to both client and horse. Focusing on the 'success' of the horse submitting and 'joining-up' with them, rather than the *process* of the person and horse simultaneously *releasing emotionally*, prevents the client from gaining awareness of their authentic feelings. It also precludes the client from benefiting from some genuine, and often much needed, somatic stress relief.

Skilled Facilitators as Conduits for this Work

Facilitators of this work are dealt a complex and paradoxical hand. On the one hand, they need to be highly trained, skilled and experienced; many will also have other professional qualifications. But equally, in order to let the horses work, they often need to interfere minimally in the process while also providing a huge amount of support or 'holding' for their clients. This is sometimes hard to convey, but essentially, equine facilitated practitioners need to be able to skillfully facilitate *and* step out of the way to allow the horse and client's process to unfold. Having horses present therefore adds a whole other dimension to a learning or therapeutic process. It is not all about the role of the therapist or coach; they need to be able to both facilitate *and* allow the horse to work. This then requires an unusual set of skills that will not come naturally to everybody wishing to do this work.

I find that this method works best when, as the practitioner, we can both skillfully facilitate *and* act as the conduit for the process where we create and hold the space for the horse and client to engage. A conduit *allows or enables* something to happen. The definition of a conduit is 'a person or organization that acts as a channel for the transmission of something'.⁶ They create a safe space for something spontaneous to occur. In addition, I like the term that Shamans use for their role, which is being a 'hollow-bone'. This is someone who continually works through their own healing so that they are clear and more able to help their clients and enable healing to occur *without* the interference of their own story.

The attitude of the professional involved is therefore crucial, and particularly central to this is their ability to trust the horses to do their job. This, for me, is the biggest element of being able to facilitate this work well; to be able to fully *trust* your horses to bring what they do so well and not try to control the sessions. Without this trust, we may as well not include horses. As facilitators, we need to be humble and sufficiently ego-less to allow another sentient being and species to take a leading role in our work together. Therefore, the training and approach of practitioners is crucial to ensure that the central true role of horses is being fulfilled *and* that the horses' welfare is being upheld at all times. It is a slippery slope to view the horses as being there solely for the purpose of completing a task with a client or group of clients or to somehow back up what you are teaching.

Where practitioners can often go wrong, is in thinking they need to *do* something to ensure the client has a successful session. They think they need an agenda, an activity or a structure; maybe even a pre-planned session where they decide which horse the client will work with on that day and what they might *do* together. They may overly intervene by asking the clients too many questions or questions which are too intrusive. They may choose to set out physical obstacles or they may have a particular exercise in mind. All of which brings their own agenda to the forefront of the process and potentially inhibits *what might want to happen* between the client and a horse in the moment. This is where we get in the way of the natural course of things *and* prevent our horses from fulfilling their full potential.

To illustrate these issues a little more, here is a real life example of a client, whom I shall refer to as Michael, who was a young man of eighteen, suffering from mild depression. Michael talks about his contrasting experiences of visiting both a horse sanctuary and undertaking some initial EFL sessions. The first example is his visit to a horse sanctuary and demonstrates the gentle, inherent healing potential of horses:

'Being that I did not go to participate in any sessions or do any sort of horse work, I was free to just be with the horses, to just be in their space without any preconceived notions about what they are doing and why they are doing it. The sense of calmness that came from this setting gave me more time to just breathe and find my own emotions. I came out of it feeling like there was a positive shift in myself, emotionally and thus physically. I found myself getting much more out of my one day with the horses than multiple sessions that had a time constraint and what seemed to be a pre-set plan of what myself and the horse in fact were going to do.'

The second example is his experience of some initial EFL sessions and demonstrates how overly-facilitating an EFL session can actually detract from the natural healing potential of horses:

'Upon my arrival I found the atmosphere to be quite overbearing and feeling rather contrived, not conducive to any personal growth or connection with the horse. Throughout my session I was told what everything meant, what I did or didn't do, or any action that the horse did; all of it seemed to have a specific meaning that had already been figured out by the facilitator rather than myself taking each action as I felt it was meant in regards to my own growth.'

Of course, there are times when it is helpful to introduce a theme or technique to help with the client's learning. However, once we have done that, if we then step back and allow the client and horse time and space to proceed, then we are enabling the horse to step in as teacher and healer.

It is also important to remember that everyone moves at their own pace with specific regard to our clients. On occasions, I have experienced a horse literally stand between me and the client if I have been pushing my client too much. These instances were driven by my inexperience, an over-eagerness to prove myself as competent, and of course, a desire to help. On those occasions, the horses were literally blocking me from the client. Moreover, they were creating the space for the client to be left alone with their thoughts and feelings *and* with the horse's support.

In the Eponaquest® Approach, we use a model called *Authentic Community Building Skills* (see Appendix 3). Inherent in this model is being able to stay present with all of our emotions even when they are uncomfortable, and resist the urge to want to *fix* others in order to feel better ourselves. When we try to fix someone else, or indeed a horse, this is always about meeting a need within us and never about what is best for the other person. Our needs are taking priority over theirs and we are not being fully present for the client.

This is why the horses will intervene if this is happening. They know who the client is, as they are fully aware of the client's vulnerability in that moment and their instinct is to protect and support the client, not our ego or professional reputation. I have experienced horses behave very differently on many occasions towards me and my clients. They absolutely know who is most vulnerable in any given moment and they can also sense when someone is being controlling. Then they will act as a shield, as in my own examples above, where the horses stood between me and the client.

Equally, horses absolutely know who their lead person is at any given time. This is especially so if we work with the same horses a lot and build strong relationships as we work together over a period of time. So I have also experienced horses look to me for support and guidance during sessions, and if anything occurs to frighten them, they will often look my way or come over to me for reassurance. This is a key reason why I believe that practitioners need to be highly skilled and sensitive horse professionals as well as having excellent people skills. We need to deftly switch between both modes simultaneously and quickly in order to support both horse and client. Further, I am of the belief that this applies equally to those approaches which employ a team made up of an equine specialist and therapist/coach.

Why Intervention is Sometimes Necessary

There will obviously also be occasions when we *must* intervene, for example if safety becomes an issue and a reminder of the safety parameters is necessary. Or we may sense a client is stuck, so we may then ask them what they are experiencing and then perhaps offer a suggestion for how they may move forward.

It takes time and practice to know when to intervene, how much and in what way. This is why it is vital that trainees and newly qualified practitioners take their time, have supervised practice in this initial period and also shadow and partner with more experienced practitioners. It can take a few years to hone one's skills sufficiently.

Here are some examples of when it is necessary or helpful for facilitators to intervene:

The first situation where I believe it is essential to intervene is where there is a safety concern. This might arise, for example, because a boundary is needing to be set, or the safety of a person in an enclosed space with a horse is a concern. Obviously, because horses are involved and they are large powerful animals, safety is our number one priority throughout and hopefully this will have been addressed formally at the beginning of the session. In my own practice, for instance, I give clients a safety contract to read and sign and I take them through a safety briefing before we begin working together.

It is important to be aware that safety may *become* an issue at any point in a session, and if so, then you *must* always intervene, regardless of anything else that may be going on. If necessary, you must stop the process mid-way to re-establish a safety rule or address a physical safety concern. Two of the most common ways in which this often happens is when a client forgets about not standing directly behind a horse or, in a round pen or arena, the person inadvertently places themselves between the horse and the fence. In those moments you would call out a reminder of the safety rule. If they do not stop and readjust themselves, then you must step in and stop things.

Addressing safety issues is obviously first and foremost for a client's physical safety and well-being. In addition, clearly and openly addressing safety issues is also a very important aspect of us, as the practitioner, *modeling healthy self-care practices* for our clients. This is often a vital contributory factor both in their own development and healing and in them learning to set boundaries for themselves. By reminding clients to keep their self-care a priority and thereby not repeat old wounds where they tend to place themselves and their well-being secondary, we are assisting in an important part of many clients' growth.

Further, letting clients discover their own boundaries and safety limits, to a point, can also be an important part of this work, if carried out appropriately. It is all a matter of degree and of employing our intuition and common sense wisely. This also depends on the emotional state of our client on any given day or a client's particular challenges. For instance, a horse simply pushing or nudging a person gently is the kind of potential safety issue that can be just monitored, initially at least, to observe how the client responds; stepping in only if the horse appears to be increasing their pressure and the client *is not* responding. At the other end of the scale, however, are the two common examples I gave earlier where the client either forgets about not standing directly behind a horse or the person places themselves between the horse and the fence; in these situations it is vital to call our a safety reminder immediately.

I believe, however, that some facilitators can go too far in respect of not intervening soon enough. I have certainly seen some facilitators allow a boundary to be *clearly* violated by a horse and *not* remind the client or trainee of their safety and boundaries. This might involve a horse moving right into a person's personal space, knocking them with their entire body and even beginning to herd them around. This can happen if the practitioner is relatively inexperienced or lacking assertiveness and they may not yet feel confident enough to step in and remind their clients about their safety. Or, it may be because the facilitator is waiting too long to see if the client sets a boundary to ascertain whether they can generally keep themselves safe or not. When facilitating this work we need to be constantly assessing the risks involved. My general approach therefore to avoid any unnecessary risks is to always err on the side of caution, and use a more direct approach in these instances through giving a safety reminder; then once the client is out of danger, we can gently explore what just occurred.

Therefore, to reiterate, where horses are involved, immediate physical safety has to take priority over whatever else is going on in the session. Modeling safety and reminding clients as many times as is necessary is of fundamental importance to their experience. It may also, at times, even be necessary to not allow a client to proceed with a session, for example, if they are not wearing the appropriate footwear. Such an action is vitally important regardless of how disappointed or angry the client may be as result. Safety is also, of course, of paramount importance to our insurance companies, for the reputation of this work as a legitimate intervention, and for the industry as a whole.

The second situation when intervention is often required is when a client seems stuck or frozen. However, this is a matter requiring sensitive discernment on the part of the facilitator. This is because sometimes, while it may not look as if anything is taking place, the client may actually be accessing some very deep or unfamiliar feelings as a result of feeling stuck. On some occasions, therefore, it is important to let the client take the time to feel *into* their impasse, as they can often access more deeply seated feelings or memories beneath the initial confusion, frustration or anger which presents on the surface. For example, a sense of powerlessness is often a core feeling that many people avoid and yet it can lead to real transformation when finally acknowledged and felt into. For a client to become familiar with their own experiences of powerlessness can often lead to a greater deepening of compassion for themselves and increased empathy towards others. However, at other times it may be more appropriate to intervene and help out a little. It may be that something different is needed to change the dynamic or energy between the client and horse, so it may be appropriate to suggest or demonstrate something, or ask a question, to move things forward.

A final example of when we must step in is when a horse is visibly distressed. On these occasions it is clearly vital to intervene as soon as possible and you may even need to remove a horse altogether. This can sometimes arise if the client's emotional state, or indeed that of another participant in a group situation, is too intense. Often, sensitive guidance, particularly by getting the client to focus on their body and its sensations, will enable the client to move through this. However, there may be times when this is not going to happen or happen quickly enough, and so removing the horse for their well-being is important and for the safety of all concerned. A horse's response can escalate rapidly and as a flight or fight animal, they may try to escape and can then be at risk of injuring themselves or someone in the immediate environment. So, stopping proceedings and removing the horse is the best and correct thing to do here. On two different occasions, I have seen a horse attempt to escape from an arena as a result of an intense escalation of emotions in a participant, and also in response to someone in the group observing the session. If they need to, horses will find a way to remove themselves physically, but this is obviously undesirable as it is stressful to the horses and can also potentially be dangerous, so it is much better to promptly intervene to avoid such an escalation.

Good Practice Checklist

Before going any further, let's now look briefly at the key elements which I believe enable us to honor the horse's true role and create the best conditions to ensure the horses' well-being at all times in equine facilitated practice. Each of these areas are explored in more depth throughout the book.

1. Ensuring that your horses are healthy and healed and that you enable your horses to be empowered partners in delivering your work together. Further ensuring that the care and consideration of your horses' health, welfare and lifestyle is paramount to you. (Chapter 15).

2. Respecting the horses as sentient beings in their own right with their own path to follow, which may or may not include supporting people's healing and growth on any given day. Allowing the horses a choice in whether and how they interact with clients as far as possible. (Chapter 4).

3. Having regard for the horses' feedback throughout is the key to ensuring the highest level of healing for the client and the greatest level of respect for the horses. (Chapter 2).

4. Taking care not to overwhelm or stress the horses. Considering how many people are assigned to each horse. Fewer people means less pressure on the horses and creates the possibility for a deeper connection to develop between the people and the horses.

5. Encouraging clients or participants to respect the horses' physical personal space and needs, as well as the horses' emotional and spiritual boundaries. Also educating clients about not automatically touching horses without the horses'

consent. (Chapter 5).

6. Using an embodied approach. Body connection and awareness is developed in practitioners and encouraged in clients from the beginning as far as possible. (Chapter 6).

7. Spending time paying attention to emotions and the roles they play; striving for congruency every step of the way.

8. Mindful Practitioners: Developing presence and being much more non-verbal in our approach. This moves you and your clients into a more horse-like state where the horses can relate to you and your clients more easily and more comfortably. (Chapter 8).

9. Developing energetic awareness. Practitioners being sensitive and present enough to be continually reading and feeling the energy of the horses, their client/s and themselves as the barometer for what may be happening around them.

10. Developing sufficient self-awareness as facilitator about the role of your *False Self*. (Chapter 8).

11. Reducing or removing agendas, activities and structure. Allowing instead for a more fluid approach, guided by the horses' feedback and the clients' pace and direction.

12. Focusing on the process of healing rather than outcomes. (Chapter 13).

13. Considering including more reflective sessions. Allowing time for the client to feel into their body and emotions throughout, rather than focusing on completing a task, thereby allowing for a relationship to develop between horse and person. Moving away from including too many cognitive activities such as talks, lectures, presentations, handouts, or getting people to work on problems in teams which involves lots of discussion and thinking. (Chapter 10).

14. Sensitively using active round pen work, or horsemanship techniques, which are respectful of the horses and teaches

clients a softer, gentler, non-dominant form of horsemanship, while also developing their skills. (Chapter 14).

15. Creating and holding a reflective, safe, sacred space for sessions. This is especially important when working with groups. (Chapter 9).

See also *Appendix 4* which contains an expanded checklist: *Honoring the Horse's True Role in Equine Facilitated Practice - A 21 Step Approach to Ensuring Happy, Healthy and Empowered Equine Partners.* You are invited to obtain a copy of this from me, which you may wish to keep visible at all times at your venue, to remind you and your staff of keeping your practice balanced in favor of your horses' well-being and fulfillment at all times.

Shortly I will be exploring the idea of horses as sentient beings in their own right and how honoring this can lead to powerful and life-changing experiences for both facilitators and participants of this work. However, before that, I invite you to sit down under the shade of a beautiful tree in the field, watch the horses and join me in reflecting on the wider mission that the horses are leading us on...

Chapter 3

BALANCING THE FEMININE AND MASCULINE: THE ROLE OF THE HORSES IN RETURNING THE FEMININE

SHE IS RETURNING AND THE HORSES ARE PLAYING A SIGNIFICANT PART...

As the horses often remind us to do, we are going to pause for a moment before going any deeper into the practical 'how-to' of this work, in order to reflect on the essence of what the horses are teaching us.

Running through this book and what I feel is the bigger picture that the horses are guiding us towards, is the balancing of our masculine and feminine energies. Regardless of gender, sexual orientation or culture, each person has a masculine and feminine part. The current situation we are facing right now in our world is that these two energies are very badly out of balance, and so here I am going to pay specific attention to how horses in particular are stepping up to help us address this imbalance.

It is fascinating to me that the recent rise in interest in equine facilitated practice is paralleled by a global movement of returning *The Feminine Principle,* or *Feminine Nature* back into our lives and societies. This movement is growing day by day to educate and awaken both women and men to the suppression women and feminine values have endured. Under patriarchal societies and systems, devastating effects have been inflicted for centuries on both the feminine and the masculine and, perhaps most pressingly for us now, on Mother Earth herself. This movement of returning The Feminine Principle, therefore, seeks to re-balance our present way of living and to shift attitudes to the planet in terms of respecting and protecting the natural environment, rather than destroying it through exploitation and over-use.

The Feminine has been cruelly driven underground for centuries and the results of this are now being experienced like never before. As children of the patriarchy, all of us have been taught to suppress our emotions, to override our gut instincts and intuitions, and to instead value the intellect, logic, reasoning and the mind above all else. Alongside this we are taught to ignore our body, to medicate it and turn it into a machine. These inhumane attitudes are now so grossly out of balance that many people are suffering from a deep mind-body split resulting in both physical and mental illness, and debilitating conditions such as addiction are rife.

Such a deeply ingrained suppression of feminine values is leading to personal and global catastrophes on an unprecedented scale. The loss of heart-based approaches to life and relationships, the dismissal of the vital role our emotions play, the mechanized lifestyles we all lead, and the disconnection from the natural world are all taking their toll. The softness has been cut out of our psyches. Utterly desensitized, we have to strive to reclaim our empathy, compassion, love and desire to help ourselves and those in need. We have to re-foster these innate human qualities somehow. We have to reclaim our own feminine principles if we are to endure as a species ourselves and rescue our beleaguered planet. And this is where it seems the horses are playing a significant role.

Parallel to the desire to restore feminine values is the growing interest in the potential of what nature and in particular, horses, can teach us. Horses innately symbolize feminine values, including: A deep connection to and respect for the body; valuing intuition and 'gut instinct'; listening and responding to all emotions as vital sources of information; to go *with*, not against, the flow of life rather than seeking to control things; allowing our healthy instinctual nature to play a greater role and significantly, on an individual and a societal level, to prioritize connection and relationship over task, goal and achievement.

Horses also enable us to become more connected to nature and its rhythms, as an inherent distinguishing aspect of partnering with horses involves being outside, rather than in a classroom, boardroom or therapist's office. Therefore, it is no coincidence to me and other writers in both fields that these two movements have arisen simultaneously at this point in our history. In addition, there has been a concurrent increase in recognition of the benefits of other animal assisted and general nature-based therapies, such as with the rise of Ecotherapy that we are also seeing.

The horses it seems are leading the way in this regard, through clearly showing us that our unhealthy love affair with power and control over nature and therefore ourselves too, through our bodies, emotions and instincts, needs to end. A paradigm shift is required in order to re-balance our masculine and feminine energies once more, as well as our distorted patterns of power that infiltrate our human relationships and our relationships to animals, not least of all with horses. A return of feminine principles and values, so embodied in this noble yet peaceful, non-predatory species, the horses are telling us, is long overdue.

In particular, the horses seem to be urging us back into a deeper state of connection with our bodies. It is through their feedback when we are disconnected and emotionally imbalanced or incongruent, that they help us get back in touch with our bodies. This is, after all, what they model for us in each moment. Further, in my experience, it is when we embrace this way of being that we gain the most healing for ourselves and society. This is why I emphasize an embodied approach in both our personal and professional practice and why I passionately encourage this as a principal way of partnering with horses. As Marion Woodman cautions when quoting Morris Berman in *Dancing in the Flames*, '*...if our experience is not embodied, the feminine will once again be forced underground.*'[7]

The core element of my work with clients and the horses, is to provide a sound, practical toolkit for bringing back a more feminine way of being into our lives. It is achieved through and with emphasis on the positive and healthy role of emotions; harnessing our intuition; reconnecting to the body; focusing on relationship over task; valuing reflective as well as active sessions with horses; building authentic communities and developing a fluid, consensual style of leadership. Through these fundamental building blocks, people learn to use emotions as information and their bodies as sensing devices. They experience being in relationships free from power and dominance, as well as the positivity of communities which nurture authenticity from their members rather than compliance through a need to fit in.

These are by no means easy things to master and take courage, practice, support and a willingness to be vulnerable. Sadly, most of us are not actively taught how to do these things. In fact, we are often taught the opposite from a very young age and our society actively discourages these principles, if not outright denies them as legitimate.

Yet these are all intrinsic elements of how horses live and relate to each other. The horses model these long-forgotten skills for us all the time. This is why I feel it is vital to enable our equine partners to step into their role fully with us when we engage in this work, so that we can learn these lessons ourselves and not inhibit their natural way of being.

The emphasis on us moving away from being overly task-focused, I feel, is pivotal to the work we do with horses. It is through their guidance, as we shall see, that we can shift away from being such a task-oriented species and move instead into deep awareness of what we are feeling and thinking in each moment. How are we relating to others, including the horses? Where do our priorities lie? In achieving a goal and external validation and success, or in being in connection to ourselves and others? I believe it is *the healing aspect within relationships that is needed in most people today*, not whether you achieve a goal or not. What happens in the process and especially within the relationship with another sentient being is where key information, learning and healing occurs. There is an epidemic presently in modern society with everyone pressured into focusing on doing and achieving at a huge cost to the relationship to the self and others.

In our work I believe we can model and encourage our clients to cultivate the lost art of 'non-doing', of just being, feeling, receiving and experiencing. I feel, as facilitators of this unique inter-species work, we hold a special role in this regard. We can help bring these more feminine qualities back into our own lives, including in the way in which we work with our horses. I encourage the use of more observational and reflective approaches in our practice to help us do just this in Chapter 10.

Prominent Jungian therapists and authors such as Marion Woodman and Clarissa Pinkola Estés, have raised the profile of all of these issues in recent years and encourage us to examine seriously what it means to be fully alive, fully present and fully respectful of all life. They advocate that we re-learn how to trust our bodies and gut instincts, to be more deeply connected to nature and all others and to understand that life and death are deeply and inextricably interconnected as part of that 'Great Round' of life.

Horses are acting as a conduit for helping bring forth The Feminine once more. Thousands of people around the world are discovering how horses can help them develop and grow, return The Feminine to every fiber of their being *and, crucially,* heal the wounded masculine within which has been equally damaged under patriarchy, both individually and collectively.

The horses are helping bring this energy through in a substantial concerted effort, seemingly trying to help us awaken through the rapidly growing movement of horses helping people. We are all part of an unprecedented and vital shift taking place in this work. Therefore, honoring the horses and this particular element, I feel, is an inherent part of our practice and role in helping to shift our consciousness *beyond* patriarchal limitations.

Chapter 4

The Horse as a Sentient Being

'Here the horse becomes more than a commodity, a beast of burden, or a vehicle for ego gratification. She becomes a teacher whose most profound lessons challenge traditional concepts of freedom and power.' Linda Kohanov.

I have always seemed to innately trust animals, including the pets we had when I was younger, and allow them to be themselves and express themselves. I am genuinely fascinated with how animals go through the world. Recognizing as an adult that I am highly sensitive, empathic and intuitive, I realize now that I resonate with animals in all of these very animal-like ways. Yet even as a small child, I instantly recognized that the pets we had were individual beings in their own right, that each had a different character and so much to teach me. I had a much deeper relationship with each of them than the rest of my family. Dogs, cats, rabbits, and later horses; I couldn't get enough of any of them.

I passionately believe that animals should have a choice and a voice in their lives. Speaking from a compassionate and perhaps more spiritual point of view, I believe that horses are sentient beings in their own right, with their own feelings, experiences, history and a role to play in this lifetime. Horses also play vital roles in our psyches, whether on an individual level or collectively through the powerful archetypes that arise for so many people. Pegasus, Chiron and the Celtic horse goddess, Epona, are but a few that come to us to deepen our own psycho-spiritual development. In the e-book, *Spiritual Adventures with Horse*, I contributed a chapter where I talked about my personal and very spiritual path back to horses during an early mid-life crisis. Specifically, I described how horses came to me in the archetypal form of

Pegasus, to guide me clearly during a time of immense personal anxiety about embarking on the life-changing journey of going to Eponaquest®.

Kohanov has written extensively about archetypal and spiritual connections between people and horses in her books, *The Tao of Equus* and *Way of The Horse: Equine Archetypes for Self-Discovery*. Therefore, I am not going to explore this further here; instead I would encourage you to read her books if you are interested in this particular aspect.

My personal, spiritual approach includes the belief that each horse has an ancestry, and they decide to incarnate in this lifetime and choose their path and the people they will encounter along the way. I have experienced what I know many others also have, where certain horses find us. They turn up in our lives at certain times and for specific reasons. Sometimes they stay beside us for years; other times just for short periods, and then they leave us in one way or another. Often, this involves them supporting our growth and learning through our relationship and experiences together. We are forever changed through the trials and tribulations of horse ownership and relationships with these loving, beautiful animals.

Therefore, it follows naturally that I also take these beliefs into my equine-partnered work where I have found that this enables me and the horses I work with, to provide deep and rich experiences for others. I talk throughout this book about giving our equine partners as much choice as possible and the freedom to express themselves and step into their full potential. In my experience, when we do so, this enables the horse's well-being to remain much more balanced. They are much less likely to be emotionally or psychologically encumbered by human emotions if they are being really listened to and respected as sentient beings in their own right.

Further, when horse and client choose each other to work

together, a kind of magic, with sometimes enormous potential for transformation, even possibly mutual transformation, can occur. I want to share here some of my own experiences as examples of just what can happen when this is allowed to unfold...

The first example comes from my first workshop at the Eponaquest® Center in Arizona. I was taking part in the Meet the Herd exercise. Each horse was in a separate pen. I walked around, noticing how I was feeling, the reactions in myself in relation to each of the horses and indeed, their responses to me. I had noticed a rather large, colored horse in the far corner pen. I immediately felt nervous just looking at this horse. As I drew nearer to the horse, my nerves grew and I spent the least amount of time possible standing outside his pen. I began to walk away and as I did so, this large horse stretched his giraffe-like neck over the top rail, reached for his head collar, tossed it up and down several times in the air and then threw it at me. The head collar landed on the ground by my feet. Despite my nerves, I had to laugh at this undeniable act by this horse and so I allowed myself to voice my honest reaction. I said to the facilitator,

'Okay, this horse has definitely chosen me, and despite my fears, I will work with him.'

It turned out to be one of the most important interactions with a horse in my life. Too nervous to go in the round pen alone with him due to his size, I asked my facilitator to come in with me. This stunning horse called Telluride (Telly for short) and I then did a tentative dance around the outer edge of the pen; I was trying to avoid him, quite honestly. After a while, he took over and walked directly towards me, then brushed past me, gently, but close and firmly enough to give me a bit of a knock. Now my nerves really kicked in. My facilitator quietly asked me if I felt okay with what just happened.

I replied, 'Yes I think so... erm no, not really, he just sort of

45

walked into me.'

She then reminded me how to use the boundary stick to set a boundary with this horse on his next approach, which I did just about manage to do and this time, avoid him making contact with me. I left the round pen shaken and vulnerable, yet I also knew that something momentous had happened to me on a deeply personal level. Up until this point in my life, I did not even know what a boundary was, let alone how to set one. I have since realized that as a child, my boundaries were repeatedly invaded and my self-confidence to protect myself was almost non-existent. I had been an easy target at home and at school; now I knew why.

Subsequently, I consciously worked on this developmental need to learn how to establish my need for personal space and safety and I also gained tremendous confidence in working with the horses because of this. I went on to adore Telly and from that point forward, I had no nerves around him and soon discovered what a powerful healer he was for so many people.

His is a fascinating story about a wounded healer, or Shaman Horse, helping people. Telly was bred to be a top-level dressage horse. However, out in the field one day, he was struck by lightning and since then could not be ridden. As a result of this, he began to partner his owner, Shelley Rosenberg, an Advanced Eponaquest® Instructor, in her equine facilitated work. Ask anyone who went to the Eponaquest® Center and I'm sure they will have a Telly story to impart. Personally, I am eternally grateful to this horse, for choosing me that day so blatantly and humorously that I couldn't *not* work with him, and to the staff, for allowing the horses to have a choice in who to work with.

I remember vividly a further significant personal turning point for me during another Meet the Herd session at Eponaquest® where I chose a huge 17.3hh Dutch Warmblood Grand Prix dressage mare called Laramie.

Laramie was also owned by Shelley Rosenberg, who asked

me with raised eyebrows, 'Are you sure? You *do* know who that is, don't you?'

Shelley was asking because her experience of me until that point had been one of shyness and timidity around the horses, so she was naturally a little concerned about me being in a round pen with Laramie, loose. Laramie could be a handful on the ground with anyone, including Shelley. However, during those moments standing outside of her pen, as I looked at Laramie, I remember cocking my head and saying to her: *I remember you.* Inexplicably, in rational terms, I felt I *did* know this horse, from long, long ago. Yet we had never met properly until this day. Laramie and I met each other's gaze and I felt a surge of power returning inside me.

I then had a further flash of memory of when I was a fairly brave rider as a teenager and of another bay mare called Cherry, who was also deemed a handful, but I adored her and we had a huge amount of fun together. In that moment, I knew Laramie and I would have fun and I knew I needed to grow in power and self-belief. Sure enough, we had an active session together in the round pen which was fantastic fun and exhilarating. I then even went on to ride Laramie a number of times, as we had established (or maybe reawakened) a really deep connection between us.

So had the facilitator chosen my horse for me, or if Shelley had said Laramie was unsuitable for me on that occasion, I would not have accessed an immense amount of personal confidence and power that day. Furthermore, I would not have advanced in the empowered way that I did in terms of my self-confidence, my horsemanship and my equine facilitated work.

Finding My Own Horse, or Rather, My Horse Finding Me...

By far the most powerful and moving experience I have had of a horse finding me, and which makes me fully believe in horses being on their own spiritual path, was that concerning the first

47

ever horse that I owned, a gelding called North Star. Our coming together was remarkable and will stay with me forever. In our brief time together, I gained huge amounts of confidence through being with North. Equally, he returned to being the empowered, wonderful teacher that he innately was too.

After completing my EFL training, I had started the search for a horse of my own; finally, at the age of thirty-seven, I was able to have my own horse. After viewing a few horses who hadn't felt quite right, a friend told me about a racehorse who had appeared on a local racing yard from Ireland and that he was destined to be slaughtered very soon if no one wanted to buy him. Being twelve years old, he was very long in the tooth for the racing industry, so it wasn't looking hopeful for him. While my friend was still on the phone with the groom at the yard, she described him to me as a 16.1hh bay Thoroughbred gelding. I asked what his name was and she gave me his formal racing name.

On a deeply intuitive level, I immediately knew North was to be my horse just from this brief description. I even knew that his racing name was not his true name. Rather it had been given to him in this lifetime and merely served its purpose in the racing industry to identify him.

'That's not his name,' I replied swiftly, knowing with an uncanny certainty that it was not his *true* name. I knew without a doubt that this was my horse and so I arranged to see him the very next day. I bought this horse who was skin and bones, having been kept deliberately underweight for most of his life. His withers and croup were pronounced and his ribs were fully visible, the sight of which jarred against the overly developed muscles of his hindquarters. He was obviously very sore on his withers, too, from ill-fitting saddles.

Soon after buying him I asked a friend who is a shamanic practitioner to connect with him to ask him what his real name was. Sure enough, he told her his real name; it was North Star.

When she asked him why, he simply replied,

'Because I am the Way.'

For those who don't know, one of the phrases that came out of Eponaquest® in the early years was 'The Way of the Horse.' In fact, this is the literal translation of Kohanov's first pivotal book, *The Tao of Equus*. So when I heard North say this to me, it was absolute confirmation that he had come to me at this time to carry out our equine facilitated work together.

North then proceeded to connect with me on a spiritual level, too. By this point I had undertaken quite a bit of shamanic training and practice and so was familiar with the practice of *journeying* to connect with others at the soul level. So when, one morning not long after I bought North, I woke up hearing a message concerning him, I was not at all surprised. The message simply said, 'North Star wants you to journey to him.' So, later that day, I set myself time to do a journey and connected with North.

In the journey, North was simply standing looking directly at me, as if he was waiting for me and really keen to connect.

I spoke first and, filled with years of pent-up emotion at finally meeting my own horse, I said, 'I've been waiting for you.'

He replied, 'I know. And I've been waiting for you.'

Once I got him home to the livery yard where I planned to keep him, he proceeded to slowly recover, having enough food, turnout and company, probably for the first time in his life. I began to help his body recover through gentle physiotherapy and exercises and basically let him rest and just be a horse. This gentle but strong gelding showed many signs of being in poor condition emotionally and psychologically as well as physically. He was easily dominated by the two youngsters he was turned out with and became frantic when he was separated from them, even for a few moments. He also seemed pretty dissociated, as if parts of him were missing. In Shamanism this is called Soul Loss and later I was to employ a shamanic healer to help North recover his lost parts. It transpired that he frequently lost parts of himself when moved to a new yard or when separated from his herd buddies, as a way of coping with the many frequent changes in his life. Such traumatic experiences are the norm for racehorses, competition and indeed most horses, where they are routinely separated, moved from place to place, owner to owner, and face being destroyed. When no longer financially viable, they are deemed to have no 'purpose' if lame, old, or just not good enough for purpose.

When I acquired my other two horses just two months later in order to start my EFL business, I moved North to my new venue and he again dissociated and needed further healing. He proceeded to be bossed around by my mare, Connie, who was actually still fairly young herself and usually the bottom of the herd. For Connie to be above North in the pecking order, showed me just how lacking in his own power he was at that point. However, as the weeks and months went by and North was helped by me and the shamanic practitioner, plus plenty of grass and a good healthy feed each day, he began to gain weight and settle into himself. I also noticed at some point that he was able to move both of the mares around and eventually, he became the lead horse in that herd of three for most of the time.

North then had a good six months purely focused on his healing and recovery and I was not riding him. In fact, I didn't sit on his back for a full year after I got him as I wanted him to properly rest from all the riding he had done and allow his body to heal and strengthen. However, he did show a clear interest in working with people in a therapeutic manner. In fact, he was often the first one that stepped forward in sessions and, being striking to look at, he easily caught people's eye. He was a pure Thoroughbred and a beautiful chocolate-colored bay with black legs, mane and tail and a very gentle eye.

North was something of a paradoxical horse. He had survived

to the age of twelve in an industry that usually disposes of their horses much earlier, because he had been such a 'good boy' and he had helped train or 'pony' the younger racehorses. Almost anyone could ride him, he was so safe under saddle. Yet he was adamant about not being touched on certain parts of his body and would seriously warn you if you missed his early cues. When eating, he would ferociously kick out with his hind legs at horses or people that went near him. Requiring a firm yet equally gentle hand, he challenged people to develop a balance of strength combined with softness and love. After a lifetime of having his needs disregarded, North was now able to tell people where *his* boundaries were, when he was hungry and when he wanted to be left alone, as well as when he just wanted a really good scratch. In addition, North wanted people to be honest with themselves and with him; all of which made him a powerful teacher.

After just eighteen months, North had become a fully empowered herd leader and healer in our team. He had blossomed in confidence and was also simply stunning to look at. North had the magical combination of utter gentleness, beauty and grace, yet simultaneously he was big and powerful. He could therefore also be somewhat intimidating, as he insisted on strong, clear boundaries and emotional congruency from me and, indeed, anyone who interacted with him. He was a phenomenal teacher of boundaries and helping people to step into a more confident, powerful part of themselves. To move him loose in a round pen also required much assertiveness; while he was very sensitive to energy and breath, he also required quite a bit of energy from the person to get him going on the ground. Furthermore, as leader of his herd he challenged people, myself included, to step things up a gear and find more reserve and determination within to persuade him to move. In other words, he encouraged people to access their personal power. He also loved to play while loose in the arena. He would run after me if I invited him to, as if it were a game of chase, or we would move around in a kind of dance to music. Equally, he would walk quietly and happily beside me or simply stand still with me, immersed in a state of bliss.

North Star became *the* boundary teacher; there's one in every herd. He seemed to have an immense healing capacity and would often step forward and support someone who needed to feel and release some strong emotions. I suspect he had seen his fair share of rough dealings during his lifetime as a racehorse and he had certainly been severely deprived of food, resulting in considerable anxiety about not having enough to eat. All of these are pretty traumatic experiences that leave long-lasting after affects. I felt he resonated with people who had also experienced some trauma in their life and so he often supported them with this.

As well as being a great teacher to my clients, North also helped me enormously to develop my confidence and regain a sense of strength and emotional honesty with myself and him at all times. If I was not present or dissociated, he would let me know by nudging my arm gently, but firmly. If I was denying my needs or his, for that matter, he would pin his ears. If I walked into his personal space he would really pin his ears and if I touched his belly without first asking him and letting him know what I was doing, he would swing around and threaten to bite, or kick with a hind leg. All these were indications of his innate sensitivity but also, I believe, a consequence of the harshness he endured in the racing industry.

Taking the completely unexpected step to then have to let go of North, the horse I fully feel is my equine soul-mate, was the most difficult and painful experience of my life. Yet, in an interesting twist to this story, some four years later, just as I was in the midst of writing this book in fact, I found myself living once again in the area very close to where North still was with his new owner. Life can be both unbearably cruel and miraculously wonderful at times, and my story with North proves this. In an uncanny way, he seemed to have stayed and patiently waited for me to return. Not having planned or even expected to see him again, I had been off doing some very necessary deep, personal growth of my own and *thought* we had said our final goodbye some years prior. However, finally I plucked up the courage to go and see him, and the joy of doing so was and remains, indescribable. Who knows if there is a further chapter to our story together...?

A Practical Perspective:
Allowing the Horse Choice in Equine Facilitated Practice

From a practical perspective, regarding the horse as a sentient being in our work takes many forms. As I mentioned earlier, my preferred approach, as far as possible, to all equine facilitated work is to allow the horses to have as much choice as possible, in particular over whether to work or not and if so over which client to work with. For me, this is a fundamental element in upholding the true role of the horse. It is clear to me from all my experience that when the facilitator allows the horses to sense and direct what needs to happen for a client, this process works at its absolute best and enables healing to take place at a deeper level.

On the other hand, when the facilitator always decides which horse to partner with each client, we are immediately removing a significant portion of the rich and varied range of potential and possibilities for clients. Partnering with highly intuitive non-predatory animals gives us an enormous potential in our work to access pathways to healing that can take years to reach by just talking through issues. By removing the element of choice we are, in effect, blocking somewhat the very intuitive nature of the horse, which is so valuable.

From the clients perspective, when we remove the element of choice we are denying an opportunity for the client to begin to establish a true relationship with a horse. We are removing the important initial approach from the equation and rather than allowing them to *feel* which one they are attracted to, we are effectively setting the client and horse up on a 'blind date'. Yet it is often within that initial attraction or repulsion between client and horse that a great deal of important information can be gleaned by the facilitator. There will be clues about the client's self-belief, the role of their False Self and their present approach to relationships. It is also about *empowering people*. Enabling people to choose can be an important part of reclaiming themselves and their power. Finally, by our choosing, we are not allowing the client to learn how to approach a horse in a respectful way and to also ask the horse if she would like to spend time with them.

What is also possibly going on in this situation is that the agenda of the facilitator may be taking precedence over the needs of the client and the horse. If we follow the common approach of choosing a horse, haltering it and leading it to an arena, we immediately eliminate the horse's choice in the entire process. We have established an agenda which is entirely our own and does not allow for a relationship to begin to be formed between the client and the horse. There is also the risk here of setting up both horse and client to fail if the element of mutual selection has not taken place.

However, I also acknowledge there are of course times when it will be helpful, or even necessary for the facilitator to have an input into which horse a client works with. This illustrates the complexity of this work and also the deftness of skill that is required by facilitators to be able to discern when to lead on this particular key element.

It is undoubtedly the case that with certain clients, we may need to have an input into this choice on occasion and suggest a particular horse. An example of this would be a client learning how to move a loose horse in a round pen for the first time, or a very nervous or vulnerable client. In both cases, it would be far more beneficial for them to work with a horse who is easy to move, rather than one which requires a lot of energy, or is a dominant type and potentially too challenging. To give this person a very positive first experience of this particular activity is far preferable than perhaps leaving them exposed to failing the simple task and possibly also frustrating the horse.

Another example might be when teaching boundary setting with a very nervous client. Here again, it would be a far more positive learning and healing experience for that client to learn with a gentle horse rather than a dominant one, until they build-up confidence at setting their boundaries. This input may also apply if you have any young horses in your herd, or any particularly sensitive or advanced horses. Here, you may need to steer clients to or from certain horses, or in fact choose a particular horse as in the examples above.

So, there will be times when, as facilitators, we may need to suggest a suitable horse to match the particular learning stage that the client is at. It is always a careful balancing act to support our clients and horses, while ensuring we give our horses a voice in their work, to avoid the slide into 'using' them. My own general preferred approach is to always observe the horses' responses and enable choice as far as possible, only stepping in where it feels necessary. Of course, even when the horse has been 'chosen' by the facilitator, attention must be paid to their feedback throughout, as discussed at length in Chapter 2, and action taken if the horse seems unhappy at any point.

'Meet the Herd'

A very helpful exercise to use at the beginning of sessions and which enables choice is an exercise called 'Meet the Herd'. This is my preferred way to begin many sessions.

The client is taken to a herd of horses who, ideally, are loose in either a field or an arena. *Without* entering the space, the client stands and looks at the horses, while the facilitator observes the horses' responses to the client, as well as the client's body language and emotional and physiological state. The facilitator then discusses with the client which horse they are drawn to, simultaneously noticing which horse has approached the client and indicated an interest in them, or vice versa. It is a very helpful initial exercise which can be used in most sessions, whether one-to-one or with groups. It allows for the horses to have a free choice whether they wish to work with a client or not, and it enables the appropriate horse for that client to step forward, regardless of any of the facilitator's preconceived ideas about which horse might be 'good' for the client.

I use the Meet the Herd exercise in almost all of my practice. It can also be used in a whole range of settings. For example, the horses can be in their field, or loose in an indoor or outdoor arena and I have even used it with horses in stables. Although the horses' range of movement is, of course, considerably restricted in stables, they can still indicate an interest to work with a client or not. For instance, they can stay at the back of the stable; they can continue eating or sleeping; they can move away from the door and client, indicating they do not wish to work or engage; they can look away and they can look into the distance and avoid a direct connection in that way.

All of this feedback provides a rich amount of information to me as facilitator about what may be going on for the client in that moment. When horses look into the distance or even seemingly straight through the client, this indicates to me that the person is not fully present or congruent. This is usually uncovered when we then discuss what they are aware of feeling in their body. In such a situation, clients often report feeling very little, if anything, which is often an indication of incongruence. When this happens, it also provides me with valuable information about how the client then interprets the horse's behavior towards them. I find that is it is actually very common for the client to have misinterpreted the horse's reaction, both through missing real indications of interest from a horse, and through misinterpreting the horse's disinterest. This is because when horses look into the distance or close their eyes, they are seemingly resting, but they can actually be *avoiding* the person. The client will often say things like: 'They were really looking at me', or: 'They didn't seem interested'. The latter is usually, in fact, more accurate. The former is a potential indication of the person's experience of how they perceive others taking an interest in them, or not. This confusion can often then serve as a starting point to lead us into exploring further self-beliefs around how likeable the client feels they are and also what projections they are engaging in with relation to the horse, for example, 'the horse seems sad, in pain or angry.'

It can also be valuable to extend the Meet the Herd exercise and enable clients to spend time sitting while they connect more deeply with themselves in the vicinity of loose horses. However, I must stress here that with regard to most clients it is preferable that they do not occupy the same space as the herd of loose horses. There *must* be a barrier between the people and the horses for safety reasons. I tend not to do this exercise with the majority of clients, and particularly vulnerable clients, sitting directly in the field or arena with the horses; I would only do this with advanced clients or trainees and horses I know very well. I am emphasizing this as it seems to have become another worrying trend recently in both some areas of equine facilitated practice and horsemanship approaches, to have groups of clients or trainees sitting or even lying down in fields and spaces with loose horses. This is not safe and neither does it really enable the client to learn to fully focus on themselves, as part of their focus has to remain on the external at all times. Whereas when sitting the other side of a fence, the person can fully and safely immerse themselves in their own feelings, thoughts and experience.

I was facilitating this type of session on one occasion where the participants in a group workshop had a chair and were sitting outside the arena, with a notebook, quietly tuning into their bodies, thoughts and feelings and then wrote about whatever was coming up in their awareness. One client was having a particularly vivid memory about a very emotional and sad experience from a few years back. My horses were loose within the large outdoor arena when North Star came over to the corner nearest to where the client was sitting on the other side of the fence. He purposefully moved the two mares out of the way and fully occupied that space, keeping the mares away. He then proceeded to lick, chew and yawn and stand beside this client as they cried and wrote. North stood there for a considerable time, like a large sentinel, guarding them and holding the space for them. It was as if he was supporting this person by just standing there. I was watching North, but of course had no idea what was going on at that moment for the client. It was later, as we discussed the experience, that the client shared what they had been feeling. They reported that their experience of North was amazing, supportive and healing as they felt into a painful memory. North had supported this client through his own choice and to the point that he had even rearranged the herd, so emphatic was he that he wanted to support this particular person on that occasion. So, had I put this client with another horse, who knows what might have happened? But because the horses had a choice, between them they worked out who needed or wanted to support this client on this day.

Chapter 5

Respecting the Horse's Boundaries

One of the most important ways in which we can truly honor the role of the horse in equine facilitated practice is by fully embracing the idea that horses have boundaries. This is a relatively new idea with regard to horses. Yet for me this fits fully with viewing them as sentient beings in their own right.

In the wider equestrian world this is indeed still a very challenging concept for many people. However, I feel in our specialist field we can lead the way in this area. Therefore, I hope to show that as long as we sensitively respect the horse's spiritual, emotional and physical boundaries, we can ensure not only that this work does not become a burden for our horses but also that it can be empowering and enjoyable for them and something they willingly step forward to offer.

To horses, boundaries are a perfectly normal part of their relationships and communications with each other. Horses can teach us a tremendous amount about our own boundaries too and through interactions with them, we can develop our boundary agility both for our own self-care and self-esteem, but also to engage more healthily with others, including the horses.

The Horse's Physical Boundaries

The most obvious boundary we need to consider is the horse's physical boundary both as regarding the horse's need for personal space and to what extent the horse wishes to be touched. To horses, it is perfectly normal to set boundaries with one another and guard their need for personal space as well as to come together for mutual grooming, play, rest and protection. If you watch any herd you will see this happening all the time. However, it is only relatively recently that this aspect of equine behavior has been properly considered by humans.

Much of this recent understanding about the horse's need for personal space has come from Linda Kohanov. In her books, *Riding Between the Worlds* and *The Power of the Herd,* Kohanov talks about her abused stallion, Midnight Merlin who, during their initial days together, showed her about his need for physical personal space. In fact, he insisted on having his boundaries respected before anything could take place between them, even her approaching or touching him. For Merlin, without that aspect of the relationship being established, there was no further interaction possible between them; he made that abundantly clear. Through her experiences with Merlin, Kohanov developed an entirely new and significant way of relating to both horses and people.

For many equestrians, this was radically different, as it involved allowing the horse to set boundaries with people for the first time in our history with these beautiful animals. It was through Merlin's positive responses to her slowing down her physical approach towards him and giving him the space that he asked for, including not touching his body, that Merlin was able to eventually trust her. Thus, over time, he began to heal and eventually became a wonderful teacher for other people, including me and my fellow trainees during our apprenticeship at Eponaquest®. Not only did Merlin teach Kohanov about his absolute need for personal space, but she also realized that all horses were communicating this to us, too. That is, they had been trying to, until Kohanov picked up on it with Merlin and through her curiosity, began to explore it with all of the horses in her herd.

The approach Kohanov developed with Merlin's help became one of the central elements of the Eponaquest® Approach and is called the Personal Space and Boundaries Exercise. It is taught to all trainees. This approach seems to really make a big difference with horses and I find it builds trust between us much more quickly. Thus, it is the cornerstone of all my interactions now with horses.

Here is a brief outline of the technique to give you the idea:

This method enables us to approach a horse whether in a field, arena or stable, while respecting their personal space.

When approaching a horse, notice the first physical cue from the horse that she has sensed you in her environmental space. This can be up to seventy feet away, or more. When the horse lifts up her head and looks at you, you stop, rock back half a step and consciously breathe out and relax your posture. Allow the horse time to go back to what she was doing and then continue with your approach. You repeat this every time you see a physical cue from the horse, which can be any of the following: She turns her head to look at you; she flicks an ear; she moves her body either away or towards you, or she flicks her tail. Stop, rock back and breathe out at each cue and let the horse relax and go back to what she was doing before proceeding with your approach.

If the horse repeatedly pins her ears back or turns or moves away from you, she is indicating that either she doesn't want you any closer at that moment, or you have already stepped over one of her boundaries without noticing, as they can be very subtle sometimes. Then all you need to do is take a few steps back until the horse turns back in your direction. Keep moving backwards and notice when the horse gives another cue; stop there and breathe out and wait to see what the horse does next. You continue until you reach the horse and basically employ this technique at all times and all stages, whether seventy feet or five feet away from the horse, and then proceed to use it to touch or catch your horse. If her message is a very clear 'no', she does not wish to be approached, then you need to respect that. Return to check-in with yourself to see if you are maybe masking a feeling or physical state, or holding a strong emotion, or you have a fixed agenda or timescale on your mind, which to the horses is felt like pressure. Alternatively, the horse may be telling you she does not wish to be approached, touched or caught right now; remember, they are sentient beings with their own needs and preferences, too.

Using such a technique is especially important to the horse's well-being if they are already in a confined environment such as a stable. It never ceases to amaze me how people feel it is their right to go straight up to a horse in a stable, *and* enter, while also insisting the horse moves back. Is this not like someone coming to your door and as soon as they answer they walk straight in and make *you* move back...? Clearly we can see this is undesirable from our point of view. I have to be inclined to feel that this is the same for horses. We are definitely invading their space if we do this. When I approach a horse in a stable, I do the complete opposite, only going nearer or inside the stable by using the above technique and with the horse's consent.

This is a very brief summary of the technique. To learn this in-depth process fully and effectively, I recommend you undertake some sessions with an Eponaquest® Instructor. There are many subtle nuances involved and it takes considerable practice with support and guidance to master the approach so that you are proficient at it.

For its sheer impact on improving horse-human relationships and equine well-being, I highly recommend all handlers and facilitators involved in equine facilitated work are taught and use this technique. As the most obvious benefit is reduced stress in the horses, it is the most effective horse-handling method to use at all times to ensure we respect our horses and keep their stress levels low.

I have been using this technique with all horses I come into contact with for more than ten years now and there are many, many benefits to it. But the overall advantage is that it creates very relaxed and happy horses to be around and work with. I believe this is because the horses know they can trust me, as I am listening, watching and sensing where their boundaries are in each moment. I am not simply rushing in with my own agenda and prioritizing my needs, or indeed my clients' needs over theirs. Obviously, the work we are doing with our clients is sensitive, and so this is a crucial element in both creating the right environment and being good role models for our clients around boundaries. Over time, with practice and repetition, this technique becomes effortless and just a natural way to be around and engage with horses, just as they do with each other.

Recognizing the Need for Personal Space and Boundaries in Ourselves, Our Clients and the Horses

The Personal Space and Boundaries Exercise also teaches us a great deal about our own need for personal space and crucially, how we can set boundaries with horses and people to take better care of ourselves. Sadly, our society does not seem to value our need for personal space and emotional congruency, so healthy boundary setting is not usually taught or encouraged from an early age. The result is that many people grow up unable to set clear, healthy and congruent boundaries with others. Instead, they lay themselves open to being taken advantage of or abused, developing codependent relationships and struggling to speak their truth and establish their life in a way that feels empowered and safe. Further, gaining awareness about how we sometimes also overstep other people's boundaries is an important part of our own growth. Therefore, learning about our own and others' personal space and that of the horses, leads to a vastly clearer, healthier and happier way of approaching all relationships.

For many people, myself included, this can be a life-changing experience and a very empowering discovery and tool to learn in life. This particular learning for me was hugely important, having been unable to effectively stand up for myself for most of my life up until that point. It was a revelation to learn how to say no and feel more in control of my own body and life. At the same time, though, it also felt completely natural to me when I started to explore this in great depth with all horses that I came into contact with. This was when I realized it was one of the key relationship elements that they use all the time with each other and with people and which, in my view, makes a critical difference to the outcome of our relationship with them.

Teaching our clients about recognizing *their* own need for personal space and learning how to set a boundary – and for many this is also often for the first time in their life – can be a tremendously powerful and moving experience. Witnessing vulnerable female clients with histories of abuse, and who had never been able to find their power to say no to others, especially men, are profound experiences that I will never forget. As so often happens in this work, the horses adjust their response according to the individual client and their degree of vulnerability. So for example, while with me my horse North could be quite strong in his insistence that I set my boundaries and would raise his level to encourage *me* to raise mine, when working with vulnerable and less confident clients, he would greatly *tone down* his behavior accordingly.

In fact it was through honoring North's physical boundaries at our very first meeting, which enabled me to connect so profoundly with him from the outset.

When I went to see North Star with a view to buying him, he was in a small, dark and dirty stable on a long established racing yard. The man who ran the place pointed North out and went over to the stable where he was. He started shouting at him and waving his hand in the air to push him back from the door so that we could go in. He then proceeded to hit North pretty hard on his chest several times in order to push him right to the back of this grim, depressing little box. All of this was completely

64

unnecessary and actually the opposite of what ought to happen when approaching a horse in his stable. North seemed very gentle and I could imagine that a much softer request would have been enough for him to have stepped back if we *had* to go in.

The yard owner had now gone inside the stable and was chatting away about what 'a good sort' this horse was. I let him talk and just stood at the stable door and as I did, I silently spoke to this beautiful, gentle horse. I told him it would never be like this with me and that he would always have a voice in our interactions together. It seemed important in that moment to let this horse know he would have a voice. Something in me sensed that he had rarely been able to use his voice in his life and in his interactions with people. He was, indeed, a 'good sort'; he had become very compliant and submissive out of necessity to survive in the racing industry. I later discovered too that he literally didn't have a voice, having undergone the full 'hobday' procedure which is very common with race horses. This is where the chord between their windpipe and food pipe is tied back fully, to enable them to take in more air and so run faster, although it is usually claimed to be done to prevent respiratory problems. The opposite is in fact the case as, inevitably, having no filament between windpipe and gullet means that dust and food particles continuously enter the lungs, causing respiratory problems. The risk of choking from food in the windpipe is very high, too. The consequences for North included being unable to whinny except for a faint, ghostly noise that came out as he tried, and he frequently choked on his food; sometimes seriously.

North Star looked over at me and leaned forward just enough to be able to smell my hand. I knew there and then that we would leave together and that we were meant to have come together at this time. I realized pretty quickly that he was very sensitive to being touched, probably because of the rough treatment I suspect he had endured during his racing life, but also because he was simply

65

a very sensitive horse. Thoroughbreds are bred and known for their sensitivity and yet they are put into an industry that never respects them as animals with their own needs, including their need for physical space. They are purely vehicles to make money. Yet, because I allowed him to, North firmly communicated his need for personal space whether in a stable, field or round pen. He was a very gentle and easy going horse but he also could be forceful if *his* needs were not paid attention to. He showed me and our clients very clearly about how much space he needed and liked, when to approach and when not to and, most importantly, when and where to touch him.

In addition to North Star I had two mares, LP (Little Person), who I talk more about in the next section where I explore the horse's emotional boundaries, and Connie, who I talk about more in the chapter on embodied practice. Each had differing needs for personal space and therefore I had to respond in a different way to each of them. It was a fascinating experience and I was then also able to show my clients how to learn to respect boundaries by being flexible, that is responding to each horse as an individual rather than learning to set boundaries in a mechanical one-way-fits-all approach. Each horse, just like people, has different needs, preferences and limits. It was a great lesson in being mindful in each interaction, even with the same person or horse, too, as needs shift depending on how we are feeling in that moment.

As a result of using the boundary approach in all of my interactions with my horses, a very gentle dynamic very soon began to develop between us. The horses knew they could trust me and rely on me to respect them and so they were incredibly relaxed and happy. As a result, our interactions were mostly gentle and enjoyable; stress-free and calm. People who arrived at my facility would comment on the peacefulness that imbued the fields and yard where we hung out and did our work together. This was because from the very initial approach on any day, through to catching, grooming, feeding, working or riding, I was attentive to and responded to their boundaries. The times when they were not as calm were always down to me; for example, if I was having a bad day or was stressed, or letting my ego-driven agenda dictate my behavior. But for the majority of the time we interacted very happily and calmly and mostly because of the way we interacted, it was a hugely enjoyable and rewarding few years that we spent together. In addition, because of this there was no stress prior to clients arriving, so sessions ran quietly and calmly, giving my clients space and time to feel into their own emotions and bodies and gently work through their issues on that day.

Horses and Touch

It is undoubtedly the case that for many people who partake of equine facilitated practice, physical contact with the horses in the form of touch, can be an immensely healing part of their experience. Being in close proximity with these large, beautiful, powerful animals and making this physical connection is soothing, comforting and therapeutic. It is also very rewarding when a horse chooses to come and make physical contact with a person, and can be the trigger point for an emotional breakthrough for many people. Indeed, this has been a big part of my own healing journey with these animals, as has been the case for many of my clients. It is absolutely not my intention to remove this important element of this process. However, it is my desire to bring forward a heightened degree of awareness around the horse's physical boundaries, as described at length above, and their preferences for being touched, to bring this particular element onto a more level playing ground for both horse and human. This is how, I believe, we can shift away from the traditional top-down approach to horses and respect them more as sentient beings in their own right during our work together.

Through developing my own awareness of respecting horses' physical space it has become very clear to me that most horses are in fact *very* particular about being touched. Our human default is to touch these beautiful creatures; they are so big and inviting and we crave that physical connection with them, as just described. However, it may be that part of this craving is actually also a by-product of centuries of employing horses to help us work, travel greater distances and in more recent times, take part in leisure and competitive sports on horseback. Maybe it is now so automatic that it will take much awareness-raising to bring to people's consciousness the issue of touch, which for me is the same, no matter what the species. The same boundaries, respect and permission or consent apply, whether we are talking about touching your partner, your dog or your horse.

Interestingly, what seems to happen when you slow down and really explore your approach towards horses and in particular with regard to touching their physical bodies, is that a lot of horses, most of the time, indicate they *do not* want to be touched. This fundamental element of developing a relationship is so helpful with horses yet it seems it is an area which is still ignored in many areas of equestrianism and, very sadly for me, in some areas of equine facilitated practice too.

So, how do you know when the horse is indicating they are *not* happy with being touched, either at that particular time or in the specific place you are offering? It turns out that it is actually very straightforward. Horses either move or turn their head away from the direction of your hand, or most often they put their ears back to varying degrees; pinning them right back if we ignore their first attempts at letting us know they do not wish to be touched at that time. Because this is usually *very* clearly communicated by the horses, I find it odd that this body language is so often either missed, misinterpreted or ignored. My sense is that underlying this absence of noticing the body language or overriding it, as so often happens, could be down still to an unconscious attitude based on an undercurrent of dominance. This attitude involves allowing one's own needs to override the feedback from the other party, in this case, the horse: 'I want to touch so I shall, regardless of your feedback to me.' Therefore, in the context of this work, which operates primarily through the horses' feedback, and where we are showing our clients how to develop mutually consensual relationships, this is of some concern to me.

I have also seen a number of equine facilitated sessions where it is clear that clients or trainees are not being taught about respecting the horse's desire to be touched, or not. In addition, it seems the norm in certain equine facilitated approaches to have a group of people touching a single horse simultaneously. As well as the potential stress here for the horse this also makes me wonder just how empowered the horses they are working with actually are. Are the horses instead submitting and shutting down because they don't feel safe or confident enough to express their needs?

If, as an industry, we are striving to move away from the approach which uses the horses to merely facilitate the clients' learning and more towards regarding them as sentient beings, then we can see that honoring the horses' feedback in this regard is vital for their well-being. However, if we ignore the horses' wishes then we are most definitely at risk of raising their stress levels unnecessarily. In addition, in our work with vulnerable and sometimes wounded people, we are often working towards developing mutual and consensual relationship skills through the medium of relating to the horse. Therefore, we must be consciously helping our clients readjust their understanding of what constitutes a meaningful connection and relationship. This is especially important for those who have themselves allowed others to touch them when really they did not invite or want that touch, to see that it is perfectly okay for a horse to say, 'No, thank you.'

In addition, horses often have a very clear preference for *where* they would like to be touched. For example, most if not all horses do not like their faces being touched, yet almost everyone is drawn to the horses' faces as the very first place to touch them. It is highly invasive to touch another being's face. To make this more easily understood, I often suggest to my clients and trainees that they imagine how they might feel if a complete stranger were to come up to them and instead of offering a handshake they started stroking or patting their face. Immediately, the penny drops and they understand how this can feel from the horse's perspective. Further, as a non-predatory animal, the horse's face is a highly sensitive and vulnerable place. For these reasons, I always suggest to people that they initially offer just their hand to the horse to allow the horse to sniff them, to then ask the horse, either verbally or silently, if they can touch them. Only if the horse indicates they are happy with that, do you touch, and then on the side of the neck or shoulder, which I find is the least invasive place with most horses.

A natural extension of touching with regard to horses is the long-standing, rather curious habit which still persists among many equestrians, which is to 'pat' their horses. However, more people have recently become aware that, to the horse, this is felt as pressure, rather than a positive reward or means of relating. Therefore, in fact, patting actually constitutes hitting the horse, as a pat is just another word for a slap and so is probably experienced by the horse as a punishment instead. Patting also seems to be more about the person's need rather than the horse's, and it generally comes, again, from an unconscious place in us of accepting more touch or aggression than we would *really* like to ourselves and so we treat others in this same way. Again, if we put ourselves in the place of the horse in order to be able to empathize with them, ask yourself how do you feel if someone slaps you on the back several times to show affection or love for you? Is this really an indication of true connection or is it again a more unconscious reenactment of them having experienced love as force? Such a lack of sensitivity sends mixed messages, as we must do to our horses. I feel that in the equine facilitated world, we can lead the way here by educating ourselves, our staff and our clients about other, gentler ways to connect with and reward our horses.

The Horse's Emotional Boundaries

Horses are emotional intelligence masters. They glide through the full spectrum of emotions, both the pleasant and the not so-pleasant ones (according to humans) in every moment of their lives. Indeed, their very survival depends on them being adept at doing so, as for a horse to bury, deny or mask fear is suicide. It is inbuilt into their genes to feel and respond accordingly in each moment. They are innately adept at feeling emotions – theirs and others – processing them, changing something in response to the emotion and then going back to grazing. Further, as long as their basic needs are being met and they are not being badly treated, the same applies to their interactions with humans. They do not stand in their field dwelling on what just happened, mulling it over with their herd members, or wasting valuable energy harboring resentments for that particular human, if and when they return.

Ariana Strozzi writes in her book, *Horse Sense for the Leader Within*, that, unlike many people, horses just don't seem to naturally absorb others' sensory information, including projections and incongruence. '*Unlike us*,' she writes, '*horses don't take it in. Just like other wild animals, they do not hold in negative or excess energy. They discharge it. They shake it off – they don't take it into themselves.*' Strozzi continues: '*Horses know how to be responsible for themselves. When they are not allowed this basic privilege, they suffer within the confines of the human's projection.*'[8]

However, it is very important to make clear that this is *not* the same as horses putting up with people's unconscious emotional behaviors and projections when in a traditionally restricted form of relationship or setting, as they have done for centuries and continue to do today with many handlers. In these types of interactions, horses are indeed at risk of being burdened by us with our confused emotional states and reversed sense of boundaries. Indeed, I believe this is precisely *why* the horses are now helping us: to enable us to shift beyond such unconscious coping strategies, lack of emotional intelligence, and dominance-based behaviors and attitudes.

Further, as is now being more recognized by some in this field, *if we do not* employ certain key approaches there is indeed a real risk of burdening horses and creating unnecessary stress for them when undertaking all types of equine facilitated practice. I have actually witnessed this myself over recent years and this was in fact one of the major reasons which prompted me to write this book. This is why I make explicit the issues of choice, respecting the horse's preferences and needs, maintaining excellent standards of horse care, balancing workloads and honoring the horse's boundaries.

Nevertheless, the more general belief that by engaging horses in this type of therapeutic work means that we are inevitably burdening them, needs challenging, I feel. I have encountered this belief on occasions both from clients, horse owners and equine healers and so I would like to explore this in more detail here.

For instance, I have observed some clients who are overly worried about *their* perceived effect on the horse. They worry more about the horse's well-being than their own in that moment and, paradoxically, they then of course project their feelings out onto the horse rather than face them within themselves. This detracts the client from experiencing their own true feelings. If left unchecked by the facilitator however, this *can* potentially affect the horse due to the confusing rather than congruent emotions of the client; the very thing the client is worried about doing, ironically. This is where the boundaries are not clear and it is why this misconception arises in some people with a caretaking or codependent tendency. It is similar to the client who goes to see a therapist and starts worrying about the therapist's feelings or well-being. The client can be gently reminded by the facilitator that the horse *can* take care of himself and does have the ability to do so, by moving away or towards the person freely. When the client is then sensitively guided back to how they feel, this projection can be withdrawn and the horse can carry out his true role and support the client. The boundary issue is then cleared up, congruency is re-established and the horse can work freely and easily.

What I have seen happen in some equine facilitated sessions, however, is that the person's incongruence is left unchecked and the horse is then still asked to interact, often through the use of a lead rope or through a number of people surrounding a single horse and herding the horse. This is not benefiting anyone involved as the client is not shifting old patterns and feeling their emotions more fully and the horse is restricted in his ability to work freely, give feedback and feel comfortable himself. Indeed, I have seen horses show visible signs of discomfort during such sessions, but their feedback is ignored. This is the exact type of situation where the risk of causing stress in the horse is much greater.

In addition, on a number of occasions I have been talking to someone about how I would normally work with the horses – often this occurs when they have approached me to ask me to work with their horses – but they then decide that they don't want to 'subject their horses to humans' emotions'. If someone is holding the belief that their horses might be subjected to people's emotions, then their act of projecting inevitably hinders or removes the choice of their own horses from stepping into their potential role and power as teachers and healers. They are also not fully understanding what is required of the human facilitator in this work, which includes having sufficient self-awareness, congruency, clear boundaries and sufficient skills to support their clients, all of which *prevents* our equine partners from being burdened.

In my opinion, the belief that we might be burdening horses is usually a human projection onto the horse about that person's *own* fear of being overwhelmed by their own and other people's emotions and issues. It is in fact *that* person who does not have strong enough boundaries and feels burdened by others' emotions who then feels a need to over-protect the horse. Further, people who do not move through their own emotions fluently, who cannot fully feel them, change something in response and then, crucially, let the feeling pass, will tend to be suspicious of all emotions; their own and those of others. Therefore, they will also tend to believe that others, including animals and thus their horses, are also being *subjected* to others' emotions. This removes the possibility of the others' abilities to look after themselves; in this case, their horses.

Many of these issues are mirrored in our human interactions, particularly in the work environment. In fact many of my clients have experienced such issues directly. A very common situation is where a boss constantly hints and behaves in a way that indicates that they don't feel a member of the team is up to a particular job. The boss will consistently sideline the employee and give the task to someone else, thereby diminishing their potential to grow into a more powerful person. If that situation is not resolved, it may lead them to leave the position, as they are likely to feel increasingly frustrated, mistrusted and most of all, undermined, as they are being disempowered. They are not being allowed to step into a bigger part of their self that requires them to find new degrees of personal power, requiring their boss to let go of micro-managing them and trust them, instead. This is what we can do to our horses when we hold outdated beliefs in our projections; when we regard them as 'poor things' and project our own emotional immaturity, unconscious vulnerabilities, or even disabilities, onto them.

These issues are also extremely common in the equestrian world. When we take care of our horses in a manner which comes from pitying them and preventing them from being as powerful as they possibly can be, then we could miss seeing them for who they fully are. In fact, we overstep their emotional and spiritual personal boundaries and dilute their capabilities, just as in the example above with the boss and frustrated employee.

Let me now give you a further example to help explore another aspect of these boundaries and to show clearly what I mean.

I owned a lovely, sweet mare for a few years, called LP (Little Person). She was an innately very sociable and very gentle horse, making her a dream to work with vulnerable or nervous people in particular. Every time I, or anyone else would walk into the field, she was always the first horse to come over and say hello. LP had a super sensitive radar for the slightest amount of dominance in people, making her a valuable judge of character to have around and a gentle, yet powerful teacher. Her ability to forgive, endure and let things go was phenomenal to me; she was a master teacher of these abilities, both to me and my clients.

Unfortunately, following a bacterial infection after a minor injury to her hind leg she developed an acute case of lymphangitis, which is a very painful condition associated with impairment of the lymphatic system. During the initial weeks following this flare-up I rested LP fully from all EFL work. However, veterinary advice was to encourage as much movement as possible to get the lymph moving again, and so in addition to gently walking LP each day, after a couple of months I allowed LP to choose whether she wished to work or not when our clients arrived.

However, when LP came back into work she had a very large visible scar on an inner hind leg. LP still chose to work with our clients and in fact was often the one that drew people towards her due to her friendly and gentle demeanor. Interestingly though, when people saw her scars it was evident that some people felt she was unable to cope and that she was being burdened in some way. They pitied her: 'Poor LP; oh no, how awful.' Had LP not wanted to work that day, she would have indicated this very clearly and I would have respected that and told clients that she was not in the equation on that day. Therefore, if she was there she was saying she was fully ready *and* wanting to work.

So when people felt sorry for her and wanted to take care of her in their own session, it was clear that projection was happening. In feeling sorry for LP, they diminished her scope for helping *them*; a common codependent habit where the client denies their needs for support and focuses their attention instead on the needs of the horse. Whereas what was required, was for them to turn their focus back on themselves. Their comments about her opened the doorway for us to further explore these parts of themselves and their own inner wounds, scars or lame parts. LP was then left with the space to do what she did so effortlessly and so well, which was to powerfully and gently support people to access their real feelings and to help them find their own soft spot inside, where their tears were often sitting, waiting to be released.

What was especially beautiful and moving for me to see, was a horse who had been so critically ill, now stepping forward and *choosing* to support others who were also vulnerable. I sensed as well that she chose the very vulnerable clients and those who really needed her very soft and supportive approach, as she was a lot less intimidating to some clients than my other two horses. I also personally learned a very big lesson on a deep level from being with, caring for and working with LP; that from a place of immense vulnerability comes great strength, courage and wisdom.

This example highlights what a lack of awareness and/or respect for a horse's emotional and spiritual boundaries can potentially lead to if left unchecked. It also demonstrates a misunderstanding about how horses manage their own emotions in terms of their ability to move fluidly through varying emotional states; not remain stuck in them but rather continuously go back to grazing. We have to always remember that this is what the horses are teaching us and not muddy the waters with our own confusion around emotions, and then project that confusion out onto them, or indeed our clients, in potentially disempowering ways. This has certainly been a big part of my own personal journey, as I have moved away from projecting my fears and pain out onto the animals in my life and instead, I am learning to relate to and love those parts of myself; which for me is really important growth.

The Horse's Spiritual Boundaries

If we view the horse as a sentient being in its own right, with choices and a soul on a journey of its own, we can also see that some horses have indeed *chosen* to help people develop their level of consciousness. Their role now seems to be to shift us as an entire species to a more evolved level of consciousness and behavior, particularly in our relationships and emotional well-being.

Kohanov has written numerous accounts in her books about how her own horses were clearly communicating to her that their role now is to help humans evolve consciously, as well as describing the many communications she received from the Horse Ancestors; the ancestral spirits of all horses. She has also written much about how some horses are choosing to assist and support people and to willingly cope with the myriad of complex human emotions.

It seems that horses have stepped up to help us untangle our confused and damaged emotionally conditioned states that many of us grow up developing. They are also helping us to remember, as described earlier, our more feminine traits and to bring these back into our way of relating to ourselves and others, including the horses. Additionally, they are teaching us how to balance our feminine abilities with our healed masculine energies.

It has been my experience for the past ten years that I have partnered with horses in this way, that each horse I have encountered has been naturally offering lessons and guidance to us if we are open and receptive to seeing them. There is no training as such that needs to take place for their guidance to be given to us; the horses are simply doing what comes naturally to them. Instead, it is beholden on us to be willing, humble and vulnerable enough to pay attention to their feedback. It is *our* awakening to what they are saying that is needing development and it is we humans who need the training in listening to them and being willing to learn and change ourselves.

My own horses frequently offered me support outside of their work with our clients, without any sort of session being created or expectation on my part. When one or all of them sensed I really needed some help, they stepped in and supported me. In fact, I personally would argue that all horses can and do teach us in varying degrees through their innate ability to model emotional congruence and agility, healthy boundaries and clear leadership, even if not doing so in a formal equine facilitated capacity. Many a time, I have come across a horse I don't know while out walking and had an experience of how horses identify whether we are congruent or not, or whether our False Self or our True Self is at the forefront in that moment. Either by coming right over and being very engaged, or keeping well away, or pinning their ears, any horse has the ability to pick up on and reflect our true state in any moment.

If, however, we block that channel of connection with horses through our projection of fear about burdening the horses, as just discussed previously, we continue to not see them as sentient beings in their own right. Equally, we block our own and others' consciousness development.

I have personally received information through my dreams and my spiritual practices from horses in the spiritual realm, including the Horse Ancestors, who have sent clear messages to me that they are helping humanity evolve to a higher level of awareness. Interestingly, at various times while writing this book, the Horse Ancestors came to me to clearly communicate that the horses are not entirely happy with the way this work is being carried out. This of course propelled me to continue writing with their support, as if they had come to say that they had, indeed, 'got my back'.

To respectfully allow the horses to guide us to greater levels of self-awareness, we need to do what I am attempting to demonstrate throughout: To have very clear boundaries based on the concept of inter-dependency; develop an equal partnership where the horses are allowed to express their needs emotionally, physically and spiritually, and ensure we let the horses live as natural a lifestyle as possible, enabling the horse to be a horse and not an overly domesticated 'pet'.

Therefore, honoring a horse's spiritual path in this work is vital. Equally vital is not forcing those horses who show no interest in undertaking this type of work. Maintaining this view involves having crystal clear boundaries ourselves, where we respect the choice of each horse to step into their role and realize their full potential and power.

Chapter 6

EMBODIED PRACTICE: EMBODIED LEARNING

*'THE WAY TO HEALING LIES IN FINDING A CONNECTION BETWEEN
BODY AND SOUL. SOUL NEEDS BODY AS MUCH AS BODY NEEDS SOUL.
EACH IS OUT OF CONTEXT WITHOUT THE OTHER, AN ABANDONED
FRAGMENT OF WHAT IT IS.'*
MARION WOODMAN.

Learning to regularly connect to my own body, listen to its
guidance and respond accordingly, continues to be one of the most
important factors in my own healing. In fact, because embodied
practice, thoroughly supported by the horses' feedback at every
stage, has been the primary healing key for my own and many of
my clients' path back to wholeness, it is a central aspect of all of
my equine facilitated practice.

As a result, running through my approach, like a thread that
binds everything together, is my belief that the body rather than
the head is the primary route to uncovering our truest selves.
Subtle changes in breathing, heart rate, muscle tension, nervous
system and energy levels offer invaluable information about our
true emotional state. Therefore, because horses fully inhabit their
bodies, their inherent ability to pick up on these subtle changes
is one of the main reasons why equine facilitated practice is such
a powerful method.

Of particular importance in our embodied practice with horses
is the role of the heart and of making heart-based connections.
Often at odds with our head and logical, reasoning mind, the
heart can transport us into equine territory much more effortlessly.
Many a time, I have offered as a suggestion to clients that they
ask what their heart wants, after a deluge of thoughts and doubts

have spilled out of their brain-mouth connection. The change in the horse's response when a client acts on their heart's desire instead, is frequently profound and indisputable. This way alone of connecting with horses is a fascinating element of the healing potential within horse-human relationships and is an area that has been central to my approach to this work.

Another perspective on this is the idea of the 'subtle body', a concept initially developed by Carl Jung and explored further by subsequent Jungian therapists such as Marion Woodman and James Hillman. Also understood as the energy field, this is the place where mind, body and emotion meet and where it is also possible to encounter the soul.

Horses are exquisitely attuned to all types of energy fields, transmitting information among the herd in a split second to warn of possible danger. Their attunement to the energy fields of humans extends very much to picking up what is swirling around in our subtle body and this is where much of our connection with horses actually takes place. This includes our emotional and physical state, our intention, our energy level, our unconscious, and most likely on a deeper soul level, too.

As a result, horses know how we are *really feeling* from some distance away and without the need for words, history or story. Further, this subtle layer, which is also fully accessible to people through practice and patience, can be consciously changed and used to create a deeper level of connection to horses. Equine facilitated work which fails to consciously access and develop this subtle body awareness and potential, is therefore missing a huge opportunity to connect with horses in ways they more easily relate to. Attunement and conscious adaptation of this invisible part of us and possibly all living beings is, I feel, central to developing a sophisticated methodology in equine involved practice.

This is now also backed up through science, most notably through the work of the HeartMath Institute which focuses its research on the energy field of the heart and connections to other sentient beings including, specifically, horses. Additionally, current scientific research is proving that a release of the 'love hormone' oxytocin occurs during such heart-centered interactions. As a result, the important role that oxytocin plays in healing is now being given much more attention by neuroscientists and the healing professions. Horses in particular seem to respond to love very strongly. Therefore by consciously helping our clients access their emotions and their true 'heart's desires', we can facilitate powerful emotional connections to another species; one radically different to ourselves. When a deep cross-species connection happens like this, based on love, it is utterly healing and life-changing for the person and arguably, the horse too.

All of this leads me to believe that some of the more cognitive-based methods and approaches, which are very popular at present in all areas of therapy and learning, are missing the most vital part of a person's being. Through bypassing the body and thus the place where many of our emotions reside, in particular stuck and deeply buried emotions, these approaches merely skim the surface.

They may, in the very short term, lead to some mild improvement in symptoms and feelings of well-being and can sometimes enable people to start functioning again. However, if they do not take into account the body, its sensations and relationship to feelings, particularly what resides in the heart, then healing at the core, visceral level cannot be fully achieved. People are then left stuck, as well as confused, as to why their issues keep re-surfacing.

Kathleen Barry Ingram, a highly experienced psychotherapist and equine facilitated practitioner, always placed an emphasis on body-focused work in our training. She would repeatedly tell us during our training as facilitators that it is when the experience is *felt in the body* that a real shift takes place. Healing has occurred and the memory of the positive healing experience stays with the participant because it was felt in their body.

As the body and mind then begin to reconnect, this in turn can help the person reframe their understanding and perspective of themselves and their past or current experiences; literally creating new neural pathways in the process. This is what I would term having an 'embodied, corrective emotional experience'. This work is, after all, experiential in nature. Consciously focusing on the part of us where we *feel* our experience *and* allowing our body to guide us through our completion of tasks, has proven to be consistently more effective with the horses than coming from a solely mind, intellectual, or verbal place. Embodying our intentions and goals, it turns out, can be a much more effective way of going through life, with or without horses.

Why Being Connected to Our Body Is Important as Practitioners

However, before we can begin to assist our clients to access their body and emotions it is vital that we, the facilitators, become fully attuned to our own bodies ourselves. In my experience, one of the most important factors in partnering effectively with horses is the ability to be connected to your body at all times. Being able to continually tune in to your subtle physiological state is paramount to safely working with horses and to sensing what needs to happen to support others.

A practitioner who is consciously paying attention to their breath and the subtle sensations going on in their body, is then receiving vast amounts of extra information about their own process and what is going on in their immediate environment, including with the horses and their clients. It is vital that you can pay attention to your breath, heart rate, muscle tension, nervous system, energy levels and how present you are, or not, in each moment. This takes a lot of time and commitment as well as constant practice and is a clear example of our own need for ongoing self-development.

My most important teacher in this regard was my horse Connie, who I mentioned earlier. Connie was an eight-year-old, highly sensitive Morgan cross Thoroughbred mare. She taught me right from the beginning that I needed to be extremely in tune with my body, my breath, my heart rate and my anxiety, or arousal levels. Even just leading her to and from the field or stable could turn into a major disaster if I was tense, not present and not connected to my body. A number of times she simply pulled away from me and ran away to safety, as if I were some terrifying monster about to devour her.

The reason? My body was tense, my heart rate was high and my breathing was shallow. So exquisitely sensitive was she to somatic changes in others, including people, for Connie, just holding your breath for a moment was extremely uncomfortable. Connie was my biggest teacher in this regard and from her, I learned very quickly how to stay present in my body and stay connected to my own arousal level. She taught me how to be safe and able to handle her in a way that was enjoyable for us both and did not result in me having a rope burn on my hand or a pulled shoulder.

Connie had not been ill-treated; this was simply her make-up. She was a high sensitive among a species already highly sensitive. In fact, as she had actually experienced pretty good handling for most of her young life, Connie had not suffered any major traumas and so was not in the habit of shutting down. She was therefore fully connected to her power and articulated her needs without a blink of an eye. She was pure and untainted by human hands and so was a dream to partner with, as I knew that her feedback about either myself or our clients was unimpeded by her own 'baggage'.

Because Connie was so sensitive, it also made her a fantastic teacher to our clients in learning to moderate their own arousal levels, too. She was brilliant for teaching energy modulation skills and especially at helping people begin to work with their own anxiety and somatic responses.

As a result of my experiences with Connie, not only did it embed into my very being a solid ability to modulate my own arousal levels with horses, but it also enabled me to bring this ability and awareness into my human interactions. This is an example of gradually embodying horse wisdom in all areas of our life. On many an occasion since my time with Connie and particularly when back in a regular workplace, I was able to modulate my own energy and anxiety in response to what was happening in others; most especially in my line-managers. With an inner smile to myself as I thought of Connie, I would breathe into my body, lower my anxiety and watch more objectively the non-verbal cues being given by others in a heightened state of arousal. Stress; anxiety; dominance; fear; vulnerability... could all be part of the mix. Crucially, though, this enabled me to stay more connected to myself and so less likely to be *energetically affected* by another's stress or fears; a very important skill for a highly sensitive person with a very poor upbringing in this regard. However, it also on occasion enabled me to actually help *lower* the arousal levels of stressed people around me, without them having any idea that I was doing anything in particular. By not joining them in their heightened state of distress, I gently created conditions to help them begin to relax, even if just enough to not let things escalate further.

Another benefit of embodied practice is that, when we direct our attention more towards our own bodies, I believe that we are also creating a more pleasurable space for the horses to be in. By getting to the core truth of what we are feeling, and in particular by connecting to our heart and engaging with the horses that way, then horses respond significantly more positively to us. Thus, their experiences and work with us is made more enjoyable for them and the environment more conducive to them. This all contributes to the horses being able to fulfill their true potential and to them feeling comfortable enough to then engage fully with us and our clients.

I have also found that when we are around horses and we consciously stop talking, and instead focus on our breath and our bodily sensations, the horses relax and often approach us. It is then, in that type of equine-friendly relationship-oriented environment, that they can easily support us with our emotions; whatever they are. This is the time when horses are not burdened by us, but in fact the opposite. They are relieved by our shift into our body and our feelings; we are energetically more in sync with them in these times. We are more congruent and clear and able to move through our emotions in a horse-like way with emotional agility.

I have seen time and time again horses switch-off as soon as the client, or facilitator, for that matter, goes back into their head and talks endlessly. The potential for healing has then stopped. We are too ungrounded and the horses can't relate to us so well. I imagine to them it might feel like we have suddenly became a buzzing ball of energy from the neck up, with a ghostly body which is not rooted in the ground, but floating a few feet above it. Our disconnection is felt by the horses and they prefer not to be too close to us. This is another reason why the horse's freedom to leave is crucial in this work. Not only does it enable the horse to naturally remove himself, but it provides us with the vital, immediate feedback that either our client or both of us are talking too much and we have disconnected from our bodies and probably also our feelings.

Where our clients are concerned, it can take some of them a considerable time to learn how to reconnect to their long-forgotten and ignored bodies once more. For this reason, it is vital not to rush this aspect of their learning and healing process and we can achieve this best by being fluent in our relationship with our own bodies. For some clients, this can be a very long process which must be undertaken sensitively and at a slow pace. This is vital, so as not to cause further harm or even risk any further wounding in certain clients – for example, if they have experienced physical or sexual abuse, or certain forms of trauma and particularly Post-Traumatic Stress Disorder (PTSD). Asking someone to connect with their body and potentially access deeply buried traumatic experiences too quickly can be hugely damaging. For this reason, great care and expert facilitation is required when carrying out any body-focused work. This is why you need to be adept and comfortable with accessing your own body, recognizing your blocks and knowing your own usual symptoms very well when something in you gets triggered by a client or a horse. Let me give you a personal example to show what I mean:

When I am around dominant people, my memories of childhood can get triggered. In my body this often presents as anxiety in my stomach and legs and also a constriction in my throat; sometimes my words literally stick in my throat when I feel intimidated and I cannot speak my truth. It is only through becoming *really* self-aware of these symptoms and connecting them to my trigger-points that I am able to then stay conscious when they arise and not let them overwhelm me. Instead, I am able to note them and send them awareness and compassion, which allows my body to relax enough for me to safely proceed. If I am not familiar with my symptoms and this connection, then I am blind in the moment and cannot stay grounded in my body or fully present for my client and the horses. Once you lose that connection to yourself as the facilitator, you cannot effectively run a session. Your horses and most likely your client, too, will feel this lack of presence and connection and will feel unsafe themselves.

The practice of embodied awareness enables the facilitator to also be proficient at sensing and responding to the continually fluctuating energy of the session. In this way, they can tune into the horse's and client's energy at any one moment and respond appropriately. Here is an example of how this might arise with a client and a single horse in a round pen: The horse becomes agitated or begins moving around suddenly, with increased energy. This may indicate that a client is suppressing an underlying emotion or physical sensation while trying to maintain a facade of being okay and confident. Because of this the client is not connected to their body (in other words, they are incongruent), and the horses are sensing this, which makes the horses very agitated.

In this case, the facilitator must do a number of things simultaneously: They must notice any new sensations in their own body, which will give them information about what is possibly happening. For instance, they may suddenly feel anxiety, nerves, or anger. They must be able to notice and sense the increased energy in the horse immediately and keep a close eye on the horse and the client at the same time. It is at this point – and if it is safe to do so in terms of the client's safety, your own safety and the horse's well-being – that you might gently suggest the client focuses on what is going on in their body. Generally, asking the client to step outside of the round pen to do this is the best way to procced here. This also enables the horse to gain some space and calm down. Or sometimes, if we step in the pen ourselves, we can usually calm the energy down through our grounded presence, which can reassure both the client and the horse. This is another reason why it is so imperative that as facilitators we are experts at our own somatic awareness and regulation. However, if the horse's energetic state has increased dramatically and he is becoming dangerous, then I would first make sure the client is in a safe place and then remove that horse.

Without an attuned awareness of your own body, which can serve us as a readily available and fantastic sensing device, you may miss the *start* of the change in energy. Remember that horses can respond with lightning speed to changes in their environment as part of their flight or fight response. As described earlier, Connie would go from a deeply relaxed state to a heightened degree of arousal in the blink of an eye, so I had to be *ready in any moment and without increasing my anxiety level*, to be able to modulate my own arousal and hers at the same time. So, as your body is potentially sensitive enough to pick up information in the same way that horses can, if you are fully aware of what is happening in your body all the time, then you stand a much better chance of avoiding an escalation of a situation, both for the horse and the client.

Chapter 7

THE BODY SCAN

It is a long road back from the mind-body split, especially if you have experienced trauma, abuse, neglect or just general confusion or chaos as a child. My own road to recovery began seriously when I began to really connect with my body once again in my mid-thirties. It was through finally learning to listen to my body that I began to ease up on myself and really develop strong self-nurturing techniques to aid my healing. I was soon to also learn that developing a strong connection to my body was vital if I really wanted to work in partnership with horses who are nothing less than four-legged somatic masters.

During the year long training to become an Eponaquest® Instructor, trainees are taught and encouraged from day one how to connect and dialogue with their body through the use of a technique called the 'Body Scan'. This method was developed by Linda Kohanov. The Body Scan is a way of bringing your attention to the sensations in the body and associated emotions, and it is a great technique for becoming fully present at all times. It is essential, in my experience, that before you begin to see clients, you are already adept at using the Body Scan yourself to proficiently be in dialogue with your own body and to maintain this connection to yourself at all times. Only then, I feel, are you ready to safely and effectively facilitate your clients through the Body Scan.

What follows is my own description and interpretation of the Body Scan technique and is presented here first and foremost for use by practitioners on themselves.

The first thing to point out is that this Body Scan is an *information gathering technique* which is used to notice the following:

- What is happening in any moment in your body?
- What is the most prominent sensation?
- What are the messages behind this sensation?
- What is your current true emotional state?
- How is your breathing?
- How is your heart rate?
- To what degree are you grounded, or not?
- What are you aware of coming from outside of your body – from the client or horses, perhaps?

It is important to know from the outset that the Body Scan is *not* a guided meditation or a relaxation exercise, or a way to get yourself grounded by avoiding feeling key sensations or your emotions. This method is not to be confused with the other Body Scans that have been developed, for example the wonderful but much longer Body Scan that Jon Kabat-Zinn developed, as they are usually more concerned with achieving meditative states and relaxation of bodily sensations or pain.

The purpose of this Body Scan is to gather information, give your body awareness and focused attention, and build a stronger mind-body connection; not to purely relax your sensations. It is about actively going *into* your sensations to open up a channel of communication with your body. The end result, however, is usually one of a deeper sense of well-being, relaxation and feeling more grounded. This often happens as a natural consequence of the sensations naturally dissipating or lessening through putting your attention on them, but these are not the goals of the scan... they are simply additional benefits of doing it. I stress this because I have much experience of people bypassing their uncomfortable feelings and sensations in a rush to either get themselves grounded (I call this 'grounding bypassing'), or to transcend their pain by reaching a more spiritual feeling state (commonly known as 'spiritual bypassing'). The problem with doing that is that if you are focusing on getting yourself grounded, relaxed or transcendent, then you may be ignoring and further suppressing vital information that in the moment may be trying to come into your awareness from within the sensation itself.

The great thing about this Body Scan is that because you can access the actual feeling behind the sensation, your nervous system automatically calms down all by itself, leaving you with less muscular tension, calmer breathing, a slower heart rate *and* inevitably more relaxed and grounded as a result. Bingo! Now you're in business, especially as far as the horses are concerned.

You *do* need to practice the Body Scan *a lot* to become proficient in using it, getting information from your body and crucially not second-guessing these sensations either with your mind or by using your normal way of dealing with bodily sensations. As an example, you may feel a pain in your back and rather than ask that pain for some information, you respond with, 'I'm due a visit to my chiropractor who usually sorts that out,' thereby missing a golden opportunity to allow your body to speak to you through its sensations. Further, be on the lookout for clients saying 'I think...' when asking what their body is saying. This means they have clearly either stayed or reverted to their mind for guidance, rather than their body. Gently encourage them to ask again and allow their body to speak in the more metaphorical and visual ways that the body tends to use. Learning to reverse lifetime habits of either ignoring, fixing or dulling your body's sensations takes time, practice and developing vast amounts of patience with yourself. It involves a whole new way of relating to your body and yourself and developing a two-way process where you begin to listen to and respond to your body's wisdom.

The idea is that, over time and with regular practice, you become fluent in noticing what is happening in your body at any moment. You can then quickly check-in at any point including, crucially, when working with horses and clients and get a sense for what is happening for you. After years of practice of the Body Scan, I can now check-in with my body all day-long, to notice where my key sensations are, how my energy level is and how grounded I am, or not.

When you notice changes in your own sensations, even when not around the horses or formally working as a practitioner, this is a further measure of your ability to stay connected to your body. For example, you may be at a meeting or sitting down with a friend, when suddenly you become aware of a new sensation in your body that wasn't there before. This may be anxiety in your stomach, or legs, or a headache starts, or your throat feels scratchy. This all potentially gives you information about something you either feel in response to them or what may be happening with them that they perhaps are not yet divulging to you.

Being fluent in your own body awareness is crucial when partnering with horses and vulnerable people. You have at your disposal an ever-present tool to help guide you through the subtle fluctuating nuances of energy, emotion, physical sensations and intuitive hunches that are happening all the time.

Some Cautions and Suggestions for Practitioners

Always approach body-focused work with care and caution. Make sure you are fully trained in using the Body Scan, or similar technique, and that you are fully confident about using it for yourself to begin with. Please do not start using this technique with your clients just because you experienced it yourself for the first time on a workshop! A fully trained and experienced Eponaquest® Instructor, or someone fully trained by an experienced Eponaquest® Instructor in this method can teach you how to use the Body Scan for yourself and your clients if appropriate.

As the full Body Scan is not always suitable for certain clients, or at certain times, I have also included some suggestions for shorter, alternative versions to the full-length Body Scan in *Appendix 1*.

When introducing yourself and your clients to the Body Scan, take things slowly and adapt it to clients so that it is appropriate, for example when working with children, young people and those with severe symptoms or history of dissociation due to trauma, abuse, addiction or eating disorders. Even if these issues are not made known to you before you have started, be aware that we have all experienced some trauma in our lives. Even those who do not present in the above categories may well discover deeply hidden wounds once they start exploring what their body is holding on to *and* once the horses are involved.

Since I am not a trauma expert I have taken advice from colleagues to write the following general cautionary point about doing any form of body work with clients with trauma:

It is advisable to use the Body Scan with great caution with anyone presenting with serious or complex trauma and particularly PTSD. Please do not attempt to work with this group of clients unless you are specifically trained to do so, or attempt body-focused work like the Body Scan without caution and adapting it for each particular client. Sometimes it is not possible to use the Body Scan at all with severe cases of trauma survivors and sometimes not at first, but later it may be possible to gradually and slowly introduce this for some clients. Sometimes, a very simple body-based technique can be used instead of the entire Body Scan. By asking a client to notice how their breathing is, or how connected they feel to the ground, will give an indication of where they are at in terms of connection to their own body and how present they are, or not. It is also helpful to ask the client what grounding techniques, if any, they already use. Seek an expert on working with trauma clients before entering into this area of work. In recent years, there has been an increase in equine facilitated programs for people suffering with PTSD. However, I would caution that even though you provide equine facilitated services to other clients, it is important not to assume you can now work with this particular client group as they require a specific and highly specialized approach. Always refer on to those you know are working well with this client group until you are fully trained and confident to do so.

I would like to add some specific advice here based on my experience of working with people who are on a New Age type spiritual path. It is my experience that people on this type of path can sometimes seek to avoid an embodied approach, and instead can prefer to focus on purely spiritual connections and 'raising vibrations'. This type of spirituality tends to give the message that the body, the earth, and nature are to be avoided and risen above. Therefore, it can sometimes be hard to get these participants to fully focus on the sensation as it actually is. Instead they might be mainly interested in a desire to achieve pleasurable feelings, or messages from the horse or the spirit world. They can have a tendency to want to *bypass* their body and especially any uncomfortable, intense or difficult feelings and instead can be tempted to seek a less physical, embodied message. My advice would be to encourage them to stay with the sensation for as long as possible, reminding them to check if it has lessened or not. It is through them feeling the more uncomfortable sensations in their body that they will make some genuine and grounded progress towards connecting more fully to themselves. The horses will pick up on anyone bypassing their emotions and bodily sensations, of course, but the more you can coach them to connect to what is going on in their body, the better.

It is very important to remember with the Body Scan to only choose one prominent sensation to focus on. Avoid suggesting to clients that they notice two, three or more sensations. It is too confusing and potentially overwhelming. Besides, you can only really focus fully on one thing at once (after all, isn't that what mindfulness is helping us to do?) So in order to practice being mindful and fully present, encourage people to notice the predominant feeling and stay with that until they have completed the exercise, for example, they received a message and the sensation has subsided or lessened altogether.

Begin with using the Body Scan in its entirety, then you can adapt it so that it works for you, maybe changing the order you do it in and get used to doing it both standing and sitting. I recommend standing until you are proficient though, as it helps to focus more clearly on the body. I also recommend that you use it starting at the head and working down, rather than from the ground up. This is because this aids its innate capacity to help us become more grounded and move us out of our heads and into our bodies.

When facilitating a client, also be guided by what the client's present body posture is presenting with on that occasion. This can give you valuable information about their possible current psychological and emotional state and energy levels. Suggest they sit or stand in a way that feels right for them in that moment, rather than in a certain posture. Let your intuition guide you and don't insist that they stand in a certain way if their body is clearly in need of something different. Rule of thumb: No one style suits everyone, so be flexible and intuitive.

I personally do not recommend using the Body Scan lying down unless you are sure it is appropriate for your clients. I particularly suggest not doing it this way with new clients or with people who really need to work on getting back into their bodies and being more grounded. Lying down can make people too relaxed/sleepy and more ungrounded. I much prefer to keep people wide awake and in touch with their bodies, which I feel happens better when standing (or sitting, if necessary), and with feet firmly on the earth.

Further Considerations

The Body Scan is a way of dialoguing with your body and letting your body be a guide for you. Think of your body as a sensing device. Allow it to guide you to your true feelings. As well as helping you discover how you feel before and while you are interacting with others, or you find yourself in a particular situation, and then use your body awareness to guide you.

Before you begin the scan, I always suggest that you make a deal with your body: Tell your body you are willing to listen to it from now on but only if it gives you the information one piece at a time. This is important, particularly for the first time, as you do not want to feel overwhelmed. Don't try to change or relax any of the sensations you find; simply notice them. Remember to also notice any pleasant or neutral sensations that you come across as these can hold valuable information, too.

As practitioners, the idea is that you do this frequently enough to become adept at quickly doing a scan even in situations where you cannot close your eyes and do it in its entirety, for example if something suddenly changes when you are in the presence of a client. Much practice is required to become proficient at doing this in any situation. The aim is to be able to quickly tune into your body at any time, with your eyes open, in the presence of others, notice the main sensation and emotion and note it to yourself. Often what happens with the body is that the very act of putting our attention on a sensation and gently acknowledging it is sufficient for the body to relax, allowing you to continue with more awareness and self-connection. It won't always be possible to close your eyes and ask for a message but doing that before the start of the session, before entering a meeting, during a bathroom break, or before you are around your horses that day is always very helpful. Then it is a matter of staying in touch with your body and checking in as you need to.

If something significant has changed or arisen, I often suggest to people, especially if they are leading a session or workshop that they take a bathroom break if that is possible and do the scan there. You can employ this practice, of course, in any line of work, not just in our horse work. For instance, it is very helpful when working in office situations or business meetings, when you are around lots of people and different emotional and energetic states, to help you keep connected to yourself and stand your ground when necessary.

The Body Scan Technique

1. Stand or sit in your chosen position and close your eyes if you are comfortable with doing so. Take three deep breaths, not to relax your body but rather to turn your attention inwards and away from your mind to your body. Spend a few moments just focusing on your breath moving in and out of your body.

2. Take your attention to the top of your head and notice any sensations or images. How does your head feel? Is your mind still or busy?

3. Draw your attention down through your forehead to your eyes; notice how your forehead feels – often an area where tension is held. How do your eyes feel? Are your eyelids flickering or still? Can you see any colors or images behind your eyes?

4. Drop your attention down through your cheeks and into your jaw and mouth. Notice how your jaw feels. Is it clenched or loose? Is it tighter one side than the other? Notice where your tongue is in your mouth. Is it resting in the bottom, between your teeth, or on the roof of your mouth?

5. Draw your attention round to your ears and notice what you hear, or any feelings or sensations in your ears. Then notice how your entire head and face feels.

6. Bring your attention now down into your throat and neck. Does your throat feel dry and tickly? Is it scratchy? Is your neck painful, tense or comfortable?

7. Draw your attention down into your chest and into your heart and lung area. How is your breathing? Is it slow and long, or shallow and fast? Then move your attention over to your heart. How is your heartbeat? Is it beating rapidly, or slowly and rhythmically? Can you feel your heartbeat? (A surprising number of clients say they cannot when first doing a Body Scan) What is the general feeling state of your heart – is it soft and open, or maybe closed and protective?

8. Drop your attention down into your solar plexus and into your abdomen area, noticing any and all sensations here. Do you have any butterflies in your tummy? Does your abdomen feel strong? Or empty?

9. Take your attention further down into your sacrum, sexual organs and entire pelvis area. Notice anything you feel there, or the absence of sensations.

10. Draw your attention now back up to the back of your neck where the top of your spine meets your head, then draw your attention down your spine, vertebra by vertebra, all the way down to your coccyx, noticing any and all sensations in each part of your back. Is your back straight and aligned or crooked? Is it relaxed and supporting you? Or is it tense and painful?

11. Bring your attention back up to your shoulders and drop your awareness down both shoulders and arms, down through your elbows into your hands and fingers, noticing any and all sensations. Are there feelings of heat or cold, tingling or numbness? Does one arm feel like it's hanging lower than the other? Are your fingers curled up, or hanging down?

12. Take your attention now back to your pelvic area and then bring your focus down through your thighs, through your knees and down to your ankles and feet and also notice how

you are standing. Is your weight more on one leg than the other? How do your feet feel? Do you feel like you are firmly standing on the ground beneath you, or do you feel like you are hovering a few inches above it? Are you balanced? Can you feel the ground beneath your feet? Is your weight more on the balls of your feet, or your heels, or is it evenly distributed?

13. Now take your attention back to the *most prominent sensation* you are aware of; the one that feels like it wants more attention right now. Imagine now that you are breathing into that sensation and allowing it to expand very gently; sending it your breath and awareness. The sensation may become bigger or more intense when you do this but stay with it and don't try to fix or ignore it. Allowing the sensation to expand opens up the possibility of gaining valuable information that it may hold for us. Now ask that sensation for any information it has for you today. Be gentle with yourself and be open to receiving the information in any way. It may come as a color, an image, a song, a phrase or a word; it may be a memory, or you may think of someone or a place. Usually the more irrational we think the information is, the more relevant it is. Don't allow your mind to dismiss the first thing that comes into your attention as irrational or crazy. The body speaks more like a poet and in non-verbal ways, for example through images, pictures, feelings, memories, colors or even songs.

14. When you have the information, speak it out loud and if possible, also write it down. Then take your attention back to the sensation and see how it now feels. Has it changed? Has it lessened or intensified? If it has lessened, it means your body is satisfied that you have got the right information. If it persists or gets stronger, then gently breathe into it again and ask for any further information you need to know right now to help you. Repeat this step until the sensation has lessened or dissipated fully.

15. When you are complete, you can open your eyes fully and come back to your surroundings. Stretching, rubbing your palms together, wriggling your fingers, arms and toes and moving your feet can help you do this.

Further Embodiment Practices

In addition to the body-focused practice of the Body Scan and similar techniques, here briefly are some further ways of developing a more embodied approach, which will enhance your ability to work with horses and clients in a grounded and present way.

First, the power of tears: One of the most refreshing experiences I had during my time at Eponaquest®, was that crying was welcomed and positively supported. The phrase: 'Tears are power' was regularly used to remind us that lost power can be reclaimed through the healing release of tears. This approach is in stark contrast to our usually emotionless and emotionally repressive culture, where crying leads us to being labelled as 'a baby' and is another example of our cultural dismissal of vulnerability and femininity.

The reason for this particular emphasis on crying, however, is very simple and important: The horses respond much more positively to us when we *feel* our emotions and release them, and tears in particular seem to illicit a very clear and positive response from horses. When the tears are genuine and coming from a place deep inside, as opposed to tears of self-pity, for example, horses always seek to come closer to the person crying. The change in the horses' response is so stark that often, from avoiding a client, they will come right into their space and usually also make physical contact in some way.

My understanding is that when we cry, a physiological release occurs in our body, including in our breathing, muscles and heart rate pattern. We soften, our defensive walls begin to melt and to the horses, we seem to come more clearly into focus as we come into alignment of mind and body, as opposed to the normal mind-body disconnect that so many people experience.

The opposite state of this is emotional incongruence, which is where we resist releasing an emotion. In such a case and when the horses have a choice, they move or stay away from us. Therefore, this is a further important reason for allowing the horses' choice and freedom of movement, so they can feel comfortable themselves, and give us the feedback we need about our own, or our client's, true emotional state in any moment. Approaches which involve restricting the horse though the use of ropes or confined spaces inevitably risk both the horse's well-being and the amount of potential feedback from them.

Second, developing emotional congruency and emotional intelligence: In combination with using the Body Scan, or other mind-body techniques, deepening your relationship with your own emotions is vitally important when partnering with horses. Foremost, is getting to know all of your emotions and how you need to express them; knowing which ones you find more difficult and finding ways to actively connect more with them. If you find happiness difficult, for example, try incorporating play and fun into your life. Or, if you find it hard to allow yourself to express anger, regularly practice setting boundaries, even in very small ways. It is only by becoming emotionally congruent and more comfortable with emotions as valuable and helpful sources of information, that you can also embody and model this approach for your clients. If you have a particular block with an emotion, you will find you have clients who also have difficulty with this emotion. How are we then able to help them, without recourse to it ourselves?

Inevitably, this is an ongoing process that all of us have to undertake. Emotions have taken a back seat for generations and so we have learned from our families and communities *not* to show our true feelings. This reiterates my emphasis on the need for undertaking personal development, both during and after training and, once again, we receive clear messages from the horses about the need to become more proficient in our emotional intelligence.

Therefore, learning emotional intelligence skills is vital and goes hand in hand with becoming fluent in communicating with your body. In the Eponaquest® Approach we use the Emotional Message Chart (EMC). This is a really simple but effective tool for learning the messages behind the key emotions we all experience and helps us to learn directly from the horses, as the chart includes examples of how horses respond to these emotions.

Third, exploring the heart's energetic field: Practicing sensing, exploring and playing with the horses' physical and energetic boundaries as outlined earlier in Chapter 5, and the heart's energy field as explored by The Institute of HeartMath, is a way of connecting more effectively with horses. It can also really help you become more sensitive to the horses' energetic forms of communication and ensures that this becomes second nature to you in all of your interactions with them. Not only will you become more responsive and soft in your approach to the horses, who will love you even more for this, but it will also enable you to sense even more subtly the dynamics involved when working with your clients. You can contact your nearest Eponaquest® instructor to learn this invaluable technique for partnering effectively with horses. In addition, you can further develop your energetic awareness through activities like Qigong (Chi Kung); tai chi; yoga; exploring subtle-energy medicines and therapies such as cranio-sacral therapy; kinesiology; Reiki; crystals; dowsing and drumming. These are just a few suggestions for helping you build a more conscious connection to your body and energy field.

Fourth, silence is golden: Placing a greater emphasis on the non-verbal forms of communication and actively practicing and encouraging silent times and activities in your own daily life and your work. For example, silent walking, silent Meet the Herd activities, silent Body Scans, silent time just sitting with or near horses, meditation, journaling or expressive arts exercises in silence. The more time you spend being non-verbal, the more connected to your body, your feelings and your environment you will become.

Finally, deepening your own spiritual practice: Incorporating mindfulness, prayer, ceremony and ritual into your own daily life and regularly spending plenty of time alone in nature, getting really grounded and centered, are excellent ways to deepen your connection to your body. If you have horses, spend time just *being* with them, entering *their* space and energy fields without any agenda on your part or need to complete a task. Build in time around chores and just spend time with your horses; meditate, rest, journal, drum – whatever helps you enter a more horse-like state of being and which allows your mind to quieten down. Spend time paying attention to your body, your feelings and your energy levels. Just be with yourself and with your horses, with no aim of doing anything.

Embodied practice and living is vital if as a practitioner you are to safely and effectively partner with horses to support people. As the route to congruency, it is our best chance of entering the horses' world more fully and being as present as we can for our clients.

Chapter 8

Further Personal Development

Throughout this book I repeatedly stress the importance of continuous self-development, in addition to our professional training. As horses are involved in this work, they will sense anything in their immediate environment. This means that, unlike non-equine interventions such as room-based therapy or coaching, there is another highly sensitive, sentient being in the vicinity who is going to be mirroring and feeding-back our own feeling state in addition to that of our client's. Therefore it follows that in order to best support our clients and not impede our horse's role, we need to be constantly sifting through our own layers of development; as well as developing solid self-awareness techniques which we can employ in any moment, to enable the session to continue smoothly. So far we have explored regarding the horse as a valued partner; honoring the horses and their boundaries, and developing an embodied approach in our work. Now, in this section, I will focus on what I feel are some other key areas of personal development: the facilitator's False Self; shame awareness and adopting a mindful approach to life.

The Facilitator's False Self

One of the key metaphors that I use in my practice and which is particularly helpful when working with horses, is that of the True Self and the False Self. Horses react very strongly and negatively to the False Self and therefore learning to deal with the False Self is a fundamental aspect of partnering with horses. Becoming intimately acquainted with our own False Self is an important part of developing a healthy ego and self-relationship, and healing our own self-destructive habits. In addition, it enables us to support our clients to navigate their often long journey from surviving to thriving, without us taking personally the slings and arrows that their False Self may sometimes wish to throw at us.

The False Self, a term originally developed and introduced into psychoanalysis by D.W. Winnicott in the 1960s, is that part of us which forms when we are very young and in a defensive manner to protect our persona. Also sometimes referred to and understood as the 'conditioned self', or the 'inner critic', it can also carry some of our personal and collective shadow parts. The shadow contains the aspects of our personality which we have banished to the basement through our dislike and rejection of them, as they don't meet either our own or others' approval of us.

Viewed in this light then, the False Self houses our more undesirable beliefs, attitudes and behaviors. In addition, the original formation of the False Self's beliefs usually stems from external sources and influences, rather than from our own deep, inner knowing and truth. It also continues, in adulthood, to be the part of us which is influenced by or seeks to influence the external world.

In contrast, the True Self, sometimes also considered as our 'Higher Self', or soul, is the authentic, less conditioned part of us and which is derived from within. The True Self is generally calmer, more considered and more open to connection with others. The True Self is creative and sees potential, unlike the False Self which is inherently rigid, lacks creativity and sees only negativity.

While the concept of the False Self is not the whole story in terms of our psychological make-up and how we relate to the world and others, it can be a useful frame of reference in our work with horses who exhibit very clear feedback when we are at the behest of our False Self.

Many people I have worked with have been severely hampered by their own negative, habitual patterns driven by their False Self. Therefore, my understanding of working with this part of ourselves when around horses has been crucial. Without doing sufficient work early on in my EFL career with my own False Self, I do not believe I would have been able to work as effectively with my clients' false-selves. Indeed, I suspect this would have been a significant hurdle, as the False Self can shut down progress if left unchallenged or not gently encouraged to seek an alternative perspective. When we can quieten this part of ourselves and instead begin to engage with our True Self, we open a doorway into a much more meaningful interaction with horses. Then we can engage our more loving, positive, self-beliefs and feelings which are inherent in our True Self. In my experience, this is where deep healing occurs.

How Does This Work When Around Horses?

Kohanov realized early on that horses respond very positively to us when we are engaging our True Self through our congruent emotions and when our mind, heart and body are in alignment. When connected to our True Self, we are full of positive self-confidence, with a 'can-do' attitude and we are coming from a more soulful, heart-based place. Contrast this with when we are overtaken by our False Self and filled with self-doubt, negative self-talk and put-downs. The False Self can also make us overly confident and bordering on arrogance and controlling behaviors, and we tend to come from a more head-oriented place, with an obvious disconnection between mind, body and soul.

Horses move away from us when our False Self is in the driving seat. To them, our False Self is confusing, chaotic and full of tension and pressure, due to the dictates and 'shoulds and musts' swirling around in our heads. Our energy field must feel full of this turbulent energy too, and therefore somewhat odd, to the horses. My sense is that at times this seems to feel like fear to them and so they respond as any non-predatory animal would, by taking themselves to a safe place.

On other occasions the effect of the False Self is to render us almost invisible energetically, as we are not fully inhabiting our bodies at these times. I have seen many instances of horses behaving as if someone is not even there when the False Self is activated. Our lack of presence in those moments is hugely unsettling to horses. If they cannot leave physically they will instead do so mentally, and will appear to be asleep or switch-off (shut down or dissociate) in the presence of the False Self. Another response to the False Self by the horses is anger. They sense the misalignment or incongruence of the False Self and often pin their ears back, or can even threaten to bite.

Particularly sensitive and empowered horses, and those who have never needed to learn to shut down and block out our human tendencies to be controlling, will react very strongly to our False Self. My mare Connie who I talked about in Chapter 6 was exceptionally sensitive to the presence of the False Self. She would either completely avoid or move away from someone in this state, myself included. Attempting anything with her when in this state was out of the question. She therefore taught everyone that to engage with her required the person to first move into a more authentic place themselves.

How This Affects Our Work

What can easily happen for the human professional in equine facilitated work is that when we step into the arena or space with the horses, and especially when we have an audience, our False Self takes over. Our False Self is then more concerned with how we look, that we sound like we know what we are talking about and that we are credible. We try very hard not to look 'foolish', according to our False Self, in front of peers, trainees, potential clients, actual clients or potential funders. When people get nervous before giving a talk, leading a group or demonstrating something, it is their False Self which fills their head with innumerable self-doubts about their capabilities and potential. We hear things like: 'Who am I to be doing or saying this?' 'Everyone is going to think I am stupid, or lacking credibility.' 'What if I mess up?' And especially in relation to work involving horses: 'What if the horses don't do what I hope they will?' 'What if it isn't a powerful, moving experience? People will think I'm a fraud!'

That old saying, 'never work with children or animals', of course holds much truth. Working with either means we are in an uninhibited, more spontaneous and instinctive realm, where literally anything can happen. Unlike adults, neither are hugely hindered by a conditioned and controlling False Self or professional persona which needs to feel accepted and understood at all costs.

I think one of the hardest, yet most important tasks for people working in partnership with horses, is to be able to do enough self-development work to lessen the role of their False Self and to nurture their true, more authentic self. The True Self is the part of us which is capable of developing an aware, sensitive relationship with another sentient being, on terms that work well for both of them. When we are connected firmly to our True Self, we have a much better chance of remaining conscious, present and focused on our horses all of the time; all states which, of course, the horses love us to embody.

When we are not in the spotlight, such as when we are sitting outside the arena or the round pen as an observer, we are not taken over as much by our False Self and as a result we can see more clearly the horses' feedback. We are able to be much more objective. However, as soon as we step into that space, our professional persona can suddenly get much bigger. If we are not sufficiently self-aware *and* have a well-developed authentic self, who can fill us with self-belief and self-trust to counteract our False Self in these moments, it can then overtake us if we are not careful.

This is also where the Body Scan works in conjunction with

awareness of our False Self. It is often through reconnecting to a sensation in our body that we find our real feelings, our False Self calms down and we come back into alignment. Our True Self therefore, resides in our bodily sensations; whereas our False Self likes to take refuge in our mind and avoid the body at all costs.

Self-Awareness is Key

If we are not sufficiently aware of the role of our False Self and keep it in check, then our ability to clearly see and sense what the horses are saying to us can be impeded. It is then that we can easily ignore their feedback and things begin to deteriorate. This is most often seen at workshops or demonstrations where presenters talk about paying attention to the horses' feedback. Then, as soon as we step through the gate into the space with the horses, self-conscious doubts can take over. We are then at risk of being less sensitive and aware to sometimes even the most overt feedback from the horses, for example: the horses pinning their ears, walking away, or appearing to switch-off.

In addition, without sufficient awareness of our False Self, we will be limited in our ability to help clients move beyond *their* coping mechanisms, and often hugely self-destructive behaviors of their own False Self. Any addictive or self-destructive behavior is fueled and driven by negative self-talk, which is the voice of our False Self. As a practitioner, we need to be aware of the myriad possible voices and tactics that the False Self can use. It seems to have an endless capacity to come up with new and more harmful ones all the time. Yet without fully understanding that these voices can be both very quiet, almost imperceptible yet equally dangerous, and also very loud and obvious, then it can be easy to miss such self-destructive talk in clients.

This commonly expressed wisdom regarding therapy and

coaching holds very true in this respect: You can only take your clients as far as you have gone yourself. Indeed, more recently, quantum physics has shown us that our own level of consciousness is crucial, as this affects all other life around us. As Jungian analyst and author, Marion Woodman, says of the relationship between healer and patient, 'in the healing process, the level of consciousness of the healer is crucial'. This is why self-improvement work must be a continual commitment for anyone practicing this powerful form of personal growth and therapy. One must keep looking at oneself anew; daily, in fact. If we do not continually move ourselves beyond our own coping and surviving strategies, then we stagnate and are not clear conduits for the process between horse and client. If we cannot keep our own False Self in check, then we can both impede *our* relationship to our equine partners, and indeed the process between horse and client.

The power of the False Self to sabotage things should not be underestimated. For example, we may be showing participants or trainees in a group workshop how to move a loose horse around a round pen. Yet we may still have our own nerves and self-consciousness about stepping into the space, maybe to do with being able to authentically connect with the horse and effectively demonstrating the 'how' of doing this. If this is the case, then we are not able to help our participants learn this technique very well. What can also happen is that the participants will pick up on our anxieties energetically through the contagious nature of emotions, which can then fuel their own anxieties about trying this activity. Then, of course, a domino effect is created, which could result in people not learning how to do this effectively. Moreover, it can also prevent clients or trainees from going into their own process sufficiently to release their own blocks, due to their False Self's attempts to sabotage them and prevent them feeling good about themselves.

I have seen this happen frequently in participants, particularly when undertaking *active round pen sessions*. It seems this one activity in particular triggers most people's anxieties around being able to perform it well enough and also around being watched by others. In group workshops, this comes up all the time for participants and so the facilitators and other group members *holding the space* for the participant in the round pen is crucial. I will explore what this means in more detail shortly. Therefore, it is vital that all the facilitators and horse handlers or assistants involved, are adept at managing their own False Self in order to guide their participants through this tricky and delicate process, and not adversely affect the energy of the session.

In addition to all of this, as facilitators, we have to be able to weather the projections from our *client's* False Self. What do I mean by this? Many people we work with will have a strong and often uncontrollable False Self. People with a need for support are often at the mercy of a virulent and destructive part of themselves that wants to destroy any of their attempts to heal and thrive. Therefore, when they come to us for support and guidance, particularly in the early stages of their healing, their False Self will be in maximum protection mode. It will try to defend its thought patterns and behaviors at all costs, including trying to diminish our attempts to help our client seek a healthier self-perception and self-relationship. For example, a client may criticize us, try to diminish our skills or the benefits of equine facilitated practice. The client may also try to sabotage their relationship with us or the horses when in the throes of their False Self, as genuine relationship and intimacy is very difficult for this part of us.

Therefore, these are all further reasons why we need to be hypervigilant towards our own False Self and know first-hand, effective techniques for dealing with this troublesome part of ourselves. Equally important is to regularly nurture and develop our True Self, so that this part of us is able to counter the False

Self and make it less likely we will be overtaken by its destructive tendencies. This is a vital aspect of developing a healthy ego-strength so that we can counter the potentially hurtful projections we may face from clients, and of course not unconsciously engage in counter-transference to our client's detriment, (and ultimately of course, our own too). When all that really needs to happen, is a gentle suggestion to the client on how to respond to and deter their False Self from causing them further pain.

It takes time and patience with ourselves and others to learn to relate to this part of ourselves. But doing so in this work is vital given the horses' sensitivity to this problematic aspect of the human psyche. To support our clients effectively requires us to have an ability to cope with their False Self too and to help them gain the most benefit from the horses' reflections. An important part of this support is knowing how to gently help our clients receive this equine feedback and navigate their thorny False Self without shaming them.

Shame Awareness

Following on from the previous discussion about awareness of our False Self, a further essential awareness on the part of the facilitator is that concerning shame, as it is often a close-companion of the False Self. Shame is a painful and debilitating emotion. Therefore, it is imperative that facilitators themselves understand how this emotion feels *and* how, if we are not careful, it can very easily be induced in our nervous and vulnerable clients.

There are two main skills we need to develop in order to deal effectively with shame. First, awareness of shame needs to be fully experienced and continually worked through in ourselves. We have to know when our feelings of shame get triggered, how we react and how we can look after ourselves when this uncomfortable emotion arises in us. Further, it usually arises very quickly, hijacking our responses and ability to even continue. Therefore it is crucial that we are able to calm ourselves down in the moment and continue, rather than react against either our client or the horses.

Second, we need to develop a sensitivity and deftness of skill when facilitating others and especially in group sessions, in order not to deliberately or unconsciously trigger shame in our clients. The emotion of shame can be used as an unconscious tactic against others in an attempt to compensate for a lack somewhere in ourselves. It can be employed to demean others, especially those we hold a position of power over, including our clients or trainees, in order to give ourselves a boost. There are a number of ways this can arise. We can shame our clients through projection, for 'getting things wrong', for appearing 'weak' to us, or for lacking in personal power and confidence. It occurs through our eagerness, inexperience, arrogance, or lack of awareness of our ego, False Self and shadow. Indeed, the very vulnerabilities that clients or trainees come to us for help with, can be used against them and we can cause great damage if we are not careful enough.

By singling someone out, mimicking their 'incorrect approach', telling someone off for not following instructions, using humor at inappropriate times, or revealing personal information or history about a client or trainee in front of others, we can trigger an intense reaction of shame in that person. This is especially true in group workshops and is a further reason why experience and solid group facilitation skills are crucial to safely run group sessions. One of many people's biggest fears and vulnerabilities in life is looking foolish and being judged by others. Therefore, when people come to group sessions, they can feel additionally vulnerable and sensitive to others' opinions of them. If we are not mindful enough of how shame works, we can leave new scars in our clients or trainees which can sometimes last for years. (Please also see Chapter 9 for more about effectively running group sessions).

Therapists, coaches, teachers, managers and leaders in any

context can get things badly wrong by being unaware of their ability to shame, inadvertently or deliberately, those in a more vulnerable position than themselves. As well as the damage we can do to our clients, the further bad news for us, as facilitators, is that a client or trainee *only* needs to experience this type of behavior *once* for them to leave and never come back. In addition, of course, they will not speak positively about us to others. Unless dealt with effectively, trust, respect and faith in the person can be immediately lost. The entire relationship can be damaged and may be terminated as a result.

Inevitably, many of us drawn to the healing potential of horses are ourselves wounded healers and carry shame, guilt, wounds and feelings of lack. This of course then carries the risk of us *projecting* our wounds onto our clients, and shaming them can be one way of doing this. All of this is another reason why we need to be continually doing our own inner-healing and be supported by experienced professionals, such as therapists, supervisors and mentors. We must practice safely, in order to ensure that we do the best for our clients *and* our equine partners.

It is only through knowing our own shadow sufficiently well enough and being able to self-regulate our ego that we can keep such behaviors out of this sensitive work. The horses never shame people, which is another reason why they make such potent healers for humans. They are often the very antidote we crave in order to get some respite from our distorted human relationship patterns. Through their loving and kind but clear feedback to us, we can work through painful memories of being hurt, teased, shamed and ridiculed in our past, that create ongoing struggle and lack of self-esteem. Again, our job as a conduit for this process between client and horse is to clear out our 'stuff' sufficiently, so that we do not impede the process by harming our clients in this particular way.

Mindfulness as a Core Approach

There is a great deal of interest these days in mindfulness. For me, mindfulness encompasses all of the elements in the approach I am describing throughout this book. It is more a way of going through life, rather than sitting to meditate in mindfulness for a certain period; although that is undoubtedly a powerful and beneficial thing to also do.

Horses are extremely mindful beings. They therefore model this way of experiencing life to us in each moment and if we listen and respond to them when we are around them, they can encourage *us* to also be more mindful all of the time, too.

Mindfulness involves being present in each moment, including being aware of the ever-changing sensations in our bodies and our continual flow of thoughts and emotions, moment to moment. Raising our level of awareness and consciousness, including our energetic awareness, and being able to give another person or horse, our full attention in each moment, all qualify as having a mindful approach to life. As does being respectful of others' boundaries, including the horses, and being calm, centered, grounded and congruent. You know when you are in the presence of someone who has mastered this art, as you feel fully seen, heard and held in their presence. You can fully trust that they will not suddenly start a conversation with someone nearby, or take a phone call, or interrupt your sentence by second-guessing what you are going to say. You *know* they won't try to fix you but will instead simply listen and be with you. This is how the horses are with us. This is why we love being around them so much, I think. They provide a huge contrast to the rest of our lives and interactions and help lure us into a state of mindfulness, simply by being around them.

Therefore it follows that as practitioners of a method that involves us partnering with a mindful and present species that is the horse, it is highly beneficial and most effective to adopt a mindful approach to our work and life in general. I have outlined throughout that when we focus on our mind-body connections, then we can do our best by our horses and our clients. Attention is centered on the breath, on developing self-awareness, including keeping our False Self and ego in check, creating safe, reflective spaces as well as developing energetic awareness and skills in ourselves and our clients. Without embodying these tools, we and our clients are missing out on vast elements of potential for shifting away from task-oriented patriarchal modes into a more conscious, present and feminine way of living. Or, to put it another way: A more horse-like way of living.

Horses love being with us and interacting with us when we are:

- Present
- Conscious
- Body-aware and centered
- Breath-focused
- Grounded
- Attentive to the present moment and task
- Connected to our heart, i.e. following our heart's desire and practicing 'loving kindness', a central tenet of Buddhist mindfulness practice
- Have clear boundaries
- Not being ruled by our False Self or ego
- Mind, body and soul are in alignment
- Attentive to energy and emotion in ourselves and others
- Going with the flow of what wants to happen
- Prioritizing being and relating over doing, or achieving a task
- Somatically rather than cognitively focused.

Using the above as another checklist, I thoroughly recommend doing a review of your current way of being with horses generally and when facilitating your practice. Highlight what you are doing really well, doing somewhat okay and maybe what you are not doing at all. Then make a conscious effort to practice those areas more fully when next around your horses and your clients, and notice what the difference is. Even simply in terms of effort and enjoyment, I guarantee you will feel an improvement and your horses will love you even more for trying.

The more time you spend practicing mindfulness as an approach to your life in general, whether with horses or not, the more your practice will improve. The more deeply you will be able to connect with and support your horses and your clients and both will feel really held by you and will be truly grateful to you. You really can't lose. In fact, the more I practice connecting to my body each day, noticing my trickster-mind and reminding myself repeatedly to come back to the present moment, the calmer and easier my life becomes, both internally and in my outer world. Then, when I engage with horses it is effortless and joyful, and people seem to respond with more ease, too, as they sense I am attempting to be as present as I can with them. This isn't always the case of course, as we all have times when we are overtaken by our emotions, defensive triggers or external life events. In these times we become hijacked by strong emotional responses and are often unable to remain present. However, the more we practice mindfulness in every moment, the less frequently such hijacking occurs over time. This agility also enables us to 'go back to grazing' more quickly and easily too, thereby becoming more and more horse-like as we go.

Chapter 9

FACILITATING GROUPS

Group sessions and workshops have always been popular in equine facilitated work and indeed this is often the initial experience for many through attending taster sessions and introductory days. Further, while many people access this work to undertake individual therapy or learning, others are undoubtedly drawn to having a shared experience with other people.

One of the main advantages of being part of a group is that we feel less alone with our difficulties. We can have the opportunity to meet people with common interests and who are undergoing similar struggles as we are. It also gives us a chance to give and receive support and even make new friends.

On a more healing level, taking part in a workshop where growth is encouraged alongside our fellow human beings, can enhance our healing through a *shared experience*. We are social beings and it is widely being acknowledged now by many in the healing professions, that being connected to others is vital for our psychological well-being and health. Therefore, it could be argued, that shared communal experiences such as equine facilitated workshops can provide a fundamental avenue of healing for many who have perhaps previously felt isolated and alone with their life struggles and symptoms.

At the same time however, one of the things that group situations can immediately trigger is memories of our childhood experiences, particularly that of our immediate family or similar communal setting in which we may have grown up. Our individual historical experience of our own family is therefore often brought to the surface in group settings. Family dynamics, roles and conflict all get triggered. Suddenly we become the quiet one again, or the bossy one, or the noisy one begging for attention. Despite all the growth we have undertaken, being back in a group can catapult us straight back into our raw child-like selves. Our deepest vulnerabilities formed while growing up, and when we were the most powerless, can come rushing to the surface once more. This is why many groups and teams are often dysfunctional as these issues are often left unconscious. An awareness in facilitators of this likelihood, therefore, is essential when facilitating groups.

For these and other reasons it is therefore undoubtedly the case that facilitating groups is much more complicated than working one-to-one. It takes vast amounts of energy and focused attention to run group sessions well and safely. As well as being hugely fulfilling, they can also be exhausting and challenging at times. This must not be underestimated, especially by newly qualified practitioners. In addition, the main facilitators need to work well together, have full trust and confidence in one another and not allow their own triggered defenses to play out during the workshop. This applies no matter what group of clients you are working with, from therapeutic groups to corporate teams.

Therefore, given the popularity of group workshops and the fact that this is how most equine facilitated practitioner training programs are also run, it is worth spending some time exploring the additional skills which are required by facilitators to deliver group sessions well and safely.

Consideration of the Horses in Group Sessions

One of most important thing to consider when working with groups of people with horses, is that we must be exceedingly mindful of the amount and variety of energy the group will bring and move through, as the session unfolds.

As we have seen, horses are highly sensitive to the energy in their environment. It is vital therefore, that we can contain and manage the group sufficiently so that the group does not adversely affect the horses' well-being. One important factor which directly contributes to this and which is easily managed by the facilitators, is keeping the number of participants capped. It is not uncommon to see big events taking place nowadays with large numbers of participants and only a few horses. The approach used then by the facilitators can have a direct impact on the horses if insufficient care is taken when running group sessions.

As when working with individual clients, the *role* and well-being of the horses is paramount in group sessions. Ideally, the horses must have maximum freedom to choose to work or not, which clients to interact with, and freedom of movement throughout the day. Because of the increased numbers of participants and the additional complexities of managing several people at once, it is especially important in group sessions not to confine or restrict the horses in any way. This will keep their stress levels down and enable them to work more naturally and freely. This is also why creating the right space and employing mindfulness is vital in group work.

Sufficient consideration to the physical set-up for group sessions is also necessary in order to be able to best support your horses. Setting up a fully separate space for the people away from the horses is ideal, to give the horses a complete break at times from the people during the workshop. Further physical safety factors inevitably apply too when you have more people to keep safe, as well as take care of your horses. It is essential to have support, preferably a co-facilitator who is as experienced as you, as well as a dedicated horse handler who can give their full and sole attention to the horses throughout. (Please note: The role of a horse handler as described here is not necessarily the same as a 'Horse or Equine Specialist' which is a specific facilitator role under the EAGALA model.)

In addition, as discussed in detail in Chapter 5 on respecting the horse's physical boundaries, it is even more important to be mindful of this when working with a group of people, most especially with regard to touching the horses. Consideration of this is essential to again ensure the horse's well-being and to show them due respect.

The delicate and difficult balancing act a facilitator has to carry out when running group sessions is to manage the group and its dynamics *and* the safety of all members of the group, themselves and their horses. But, as emphasized throughout, the well-being of the horses is of the utmost importance as our trusting colleagues.

The Number of Facilitators

Generally speaking, running group sessions takes vast amounts of physical and psychic energy and so having a minimum of two experienced facilitators is always highly recommended. The reasons for this are both to share the facilitating workload and support one another, but also to be able to effectively support each individual *and* the group simultaneously.

One example of why this is so necessary is with regard to a very common activity which takes place within group workshops. This is where each participant takes it in turn to spend one-to-one time with a horse. While one facilitator stays focused on the person and horse having the individual session, the other facilitator/s will be supporting the group members as they observe and hold the 'sacred space of possibility'. Therefore, having at least two facilitators means that should one of the group members need support or become disruptive, you have someone to support them.

Creating and Holding Space

In all equine facilitated work it is important that as a facilitator you can hold the 'sacred space of possibility' for your clients. It was Kathleen Barry Ingram who created the concept and practice of, *'holding the sacred space of possibility'*, which she describes further as: *'a fully engaged form of patience which is crucial to supporting the authentic action and expression of the authentic self.'*

However, when it comes to group work this skill becomes paramount. What this means with regard to groups is that all of the participants in a group feel fully seen, heard, respected and valued through your grounded and attentive presence. This mostly happens non-verbally through your intention and energy that you bring to the session.

There is an art, I feel, to creating and holding a safe, reflective sacred space for groups. It requires much patience, a desire to allow others to go at their own pace, to not want to find solutions for others and above all, not to impose your agenda or interpretation of someone else's experience onto them. This involves minimum intervention and talking on your part and not bringing too much of your own self to the groups' experiences.

I sometimes now also refer to this as the *'sacred space of vulnerability'*, as it is in creating the right conditions for the client to feel safe enough to be vulnerable that healing and change can occur. Without this fully attentive presence, the other person does not feel safe to step into feeling vulnerable, their ego will need to protect them and therefore they probably won't access the deepest parts of themselves and their unconscious needs and wounds.

Creating this sacred space involves several steps:

The first step I recommend is creating a set of safety guidelines or ground rules for your group work. In the Eponaquest® Approach we use a *Group Safety Agreement* (see *Appendix* 2) which is based on the skills found in *The Eponaquest® Authentic Community Building Agreements*, (see *Appendix 3*). These guidelines aim to create a safe space for the group's time together and include confidentiality; being respectful of others; taking care of your own needs, and giving feedback to others only when asked for and in a way which is taking responsibility for yourself through the use of 'I statements'. This deters from the normal 'you did' type of statement which is so often used in normal daily discourse and which leads people to potentially feel judged, shamed and criticized.

At the beginning of group sessions, I run through the guidelines briefly. I also always ask participants if they have any concerns about them or if they have any additional guidelines they would like to add, in order to make them inclusive and relevant to each particular group. A useful approach to use to further encourage this is to ask each group member to make a statement at the beginning of the session where they state their name and declare that they will take responsibility for themselves throughout the session. Making this optional is preferable, however, to allow people autonomy.

In group workshops, it is often the case that as the day proceeds, these group safety guidelines can become forgotten by group members, especially if they are new to these practices. Facilitators can also forget the guidelines if they get too wrapped up in the proceedings or the practices are not yet fully embedded in their way of being. But it is beholden on us to retain a more detached role, to guide the group if things go off-track and to gently bring people back to what was agreed, through reminding people from time to time. It is important not to be authoritarian about these guidelines, however, but instead to model them through your own way of being in a group and when necessary, gently but clearly re-state a guideline that is being forgotten.

The next step is to build trust and confidentiality in the group. This is no easy task. I find that asking everyone to introduce themselves at the beginning is important. This allows everyone to feel included and to start to get to know everyone a little in order to feel safe enough to be vulnerable and able to share. It also starts to help build trust among members and to enable the group's emotional safety and cohesiveness to develop. I attended an in-depth personal development workshop once where this did not happen and as a result, I felt unable to share authentically my very personal material, as I didn't know my fellow group members and we had not been able to co-create a shared space in any way.

However, probably the most important difference with group work and an essential part of creating a safe space, is the role and manner of feedback from other participants.

Feedback Within Groups

When each individual is interacting with the horses and the rest of the group are holding the 'sacred space of possibility', the facilitator needs to ensure that each individual has an uninterrupted experience with the horse. Therefore, both during and after each person's turn it is vital that group members share feedback only when invited by each participant. Other group members must be encouraged to share from their own experience, using 'I statements' and not intrude in any way while the experience is taking place, for example by talking, or non-verbally through holding negative thoughts or judgments.

This is another reason why, as facilitators, we need to develop and hone our somatic and energetic sensitivity skills so we can sense the changes in energy, dynamic and emotion in a group. For example, if I suddenly feel irritable or tense, it may be that I am picking up on some unspoken feelings of a group member. The horses will of course also display this 'tension'. This feeling then needs to be aired through simply asking an open question and being attentive to the body language of the participants to encourage congruency at every stage. It is highly dangerous to ignore such subtle feedback, although I might add, it won't always be subtle in the horses. The aim is not to obtain simply a 'lovely experience for all' in workshops. But to strive for the more sometimes uncomfortable authenticity which comes through people expressing how they really feel to others.

It is also very important that participants do not try to 'fix' one another through offering feedback which is of a critical, caretaking or codependent nature. Allowing someone to fully feel their emotions is vital at this stage; in fact, any attempt to care-take can do more harm than good. Even reaching for the tissues can disrupt the long-awaited flow of tears and the much needed release of pain or trauma. Any word or movement such as touching or hugging someone at the crucial moment of them accessing their pain can interrupt their process. This is why we practice just holding the space, sitting with our own uncomfortable emotions, and why we have to unlearn our tendency to 'fix' others.

Wanting to fix someone else's emotional pain or dilemma is really about our *own* discomfort in that moment. We may have developed a strong pattern of feeling the need to *do* something when others are emotional, otherwise *we* feel helpless. Or – and this is very common – someone else expressing an emotion can trigger that same feeling in us and so to avoid going into our own emotion in that moment, we push our focus outside of ourselves and focus on the other person's situation, hence the rush to help them.

Let me give an example of what I mean here, as this is a very common experience many of us have in our families and communities but which, when encouraged to continue in a *space of vulnerability*, can be very harmful and detrimental to individuals' healing and growth. When a person who has just had an experience with a horse is sharing, or indeed when people are sharing within a group setting at any point, it is crucial that everyone else listens and gives them their full attention. This allows them to be fully immersed in their experience and feel supported. It is very important that people don't start sharing their own similar experiences *before* or immediately after the participant has finished sharing. It is preferable to wait until the participant indicates that they would indeed like feedback or further discussion, as they may not. Often, it is more important and healing to simply have the space to feel and verbalize our feelings and that is all. We don't necessarily need or want to have a discussion or hear others' experiences in that moment, as part of the healing process is to be given time and space to simply be heard.

In addition, other members talking, flicking through paperwork or fidgeting in any way is highly undesirable, as this is disruptive at such a sensitive moment. It takes enormous courage to allow oneself to be vulnerable in such a shared learning environment and to openly dive into one's emotions is still so rare in our society, so the more safe people feel, the more they are able to go into their feelings.

Therefore, in this work we need to practice as much as possible giving and holding the space for each other to do this. To make this practice seem easier, just put yourself in the place of a client in a room with a therapist or counselor. Now imagine that therapist talks over you, interrupts you, rustles through a folder or talks to someone else while they should be giving you their full undivided attention and regard and holding a sacred, delicate, emotional space for you. Attentively holding the space is how we ought to be regarding each other in groups. In fact, I would go one step further here and add, this is how we ought to be regarding each other at all times.

I know there have been times when I have been on both the giving and receiving end of these kinds of behaviors in groups. I have learned not to blurt out my own similar experience, as I have seen how this can disrupt someone else's experience. I have also had other group members not hold the space for me. They have perhaps shared some similar experience too soon with me, in an attempt to make me feel better. Yet all it did was disrupt my focus on myself and I felt like I was being rushed away from myself and my feelings. Suddenly, I found myself trying to listen and take in someone else's situation when really all I wanted and needed to do was be with my feelings, thoughts, sensations.

One of the most healing things we can do for one another is

to really listen and empathize through our energetic intention, which sends out love and support without having to say anything ourselves. After all, this is just what the horses do for us, which is why so many people prefer talking to and unburdening their souls to these patient, loving animals. Tribal indigenous cultures know this and this is why they regularly sit in circles and support one another in this way. It is why, in Native American communities for instance, they use the principle of the 'Talking Stick' to indicate one person is speaking and to encourage others to listen. This is a very effective technique to introduce into your group sessions and helps people build their skills at listening and holding space for one another. It is a principle that I believe could make a world of difference in general society, too. Imagine how our governments, workplaces, education establishments and families could be improved just by the introduction of this one technique?

Group Interactions and Team Work

One of the most common things that can happen when people come together as a group or team, is that some people get left behind while the more outspoken, domineering or confident members take the initiative more easily. This frequently happens when you have leaders and managers of any sort involved, so be watchful of their behavior and try not to allow them to take over automatically. Coming from a large family and being the youngest child, I experienced this all the time growing up, so I have developed a good radar for this particular dynamic. It also means I can sense quickly when certain people are not participating or are possibly feeling excluded or left behind by some of the other members or facilitators.

When leading group sessions I would therefore encourage facilitators to be on the lookout for the quieter members and regularly check how they are feeling. As well as keeping an eye on others to ensure that they are not always leading discussions or activities. If necessary, consider stopping things and reassessing how the group or team as a whole is operating so that everyone feels included.

In my careers outside of equine facilitated work, I have attended numerous organizational team-building sessions as an employee. I have often found many of them wholly wanting in terms of interpersonal leadership skills. As well as a considerable inability and unwillingness to deal with underlying team conflicts, in particular, the non-verbal, emotional and energetics being played out. There is also in our culture, it seems, a general inability to create emotionally safe spaces for people to share and grow. I have worked in a number of organizations where this type of leadership and lack of inclusivity of the whole team is the norm. The results are disgruntled employees, unexpressed emotions and therefore tensions, lack of motivation and resentments. Ultimately, it also leads to people feeling unvalued and disempowered. Sometimes it leads to people leaving a job altogether if it becomes the normal way to proceed in the organization and with no sign of change on the horizon.

We need to be very careful not to allow these same dynamics to play out unconsciously in our work involving horses with groups and teams. Instead, all that is required is to spend some extra time in preparation at the beginning of sessions. Carrying out the following three simple processes can be very helpful in this regard: First, for everyone to check-in with their body, emotional state and energy levels. Second, to do some grounding, as necessary, so that everyone is more attuned to the horses and can be more attentive to everyone else. Third, allowing everyone to have a say in what they feel would be a good way to proceed and thus ensure that everyone feels included.

Once these steps have been taken and everyone feels part of the team, motivation levels tend to be higher and things progress more naturally as people feel more connected to themselves and therefore each other, including, vitally, the horses.

Size of Groups

Size of groups in this work is very important to consider. This is for two main reasons. Firstly so that you as facilitator can effectively hold the space for everyone, not just a few. Secondly, so that the group's energy does not overwhelm or stress the horses.

If there are too many people in a session then a safe supportive group cannot be easily created and held. In my Eponaquest® training, there were sixteen of us. Most of the time, however, we worked and practiced in smaller groups throughout the training. These were usually groups of four or five people at most. This meant that we were able to experience each part in more depth and with just a few people watching us at a time, rather than a larger group and a more intimidating number of eyes. So for each element that we were focusing on, for example reflective or active round pen work, each small group would have their own space _away_ from the other groups, in order to fully feel safe to experience, learn and support one another. These are also, of course, more comfortable conditions to enable the False Self to relax and allow the authentic self to gradually feel safe enough to emerge.

Therefore, when running sessions where you split a larger group into smaller groups, I strongly suggest that you avoid running the sessions in close physical proximity, where each group can see or hear what is going on in the other group. In terms of the horses, they can easily be distracted by the other horses' movements and feelings, and in terms of the participants, it can also be distracting but it can also be potentially disrupting. If someone in another group close by is having a profound emotional release, to feel the eyes and ears of other participants who are not involved in holding the space for them, can be intrusive and potentially harmful. They are more like spectators and the person having the experience can feel 'on show'.

Obviously, it can be tempting if space is limited to try, for example, to halve a large arena. Yet for this type of deep emotional work, this is not suitable or advisable if you want fully focused horses and participants who feel wholly safe and supported. Even though it may cost more to hire a second space, it is well worth it to ensure the best experience possible for all concerned. Short-cuts are not advisable in this sensitive and powerful work, whether you are facilitating clients or trainee practitioners, as trainees will also be going through their own process.

Group Facilitation Requires Experience

If you are a newly qualified practitioner, I strongly recommend that you find a more experienced facilitator to work-shadow on group sessions, maybe volunteering to be the horse handler or to be an assistant with a small role for the first few times. Then gradually build-up your experience through watching how they manage group sessions. I would advise seeking additional training specifically in facilitating and running groups if necessary, too, especially if this has not been sufficiently covered in your training, or is a new area for you, or you lack confidence in running groups. As described, facilitating groups is much more complicated than doing individual work and requires an additional set of skills. It also takes genuine confidence and leadership abilities which develop gradually through building up your experience base. Good training providers should advise you of this and hopefully also provide you with experiences to do just this.

Chapter 10

ADDITIONAL GOOD PRACTICE SUGGESTIONS

As we continue on our path of becoming more horse-like in our practice and in ways which best support our equine partner's role, there are two further suggestions I would like to make. These involve using more reflective and observational type sessions, and developing sensitive questioning techniques.

More Reflective Sessions and Less Cognitive-Based Activities

As I have outlined so far, horses respond best to us when we are connected to our body and emotions and when relationship to ourselves and to them is our priority. Despite hundreds of years of working and carrying out tasks with horses in our care, the horses are still patiently waiting for us to catch up with them in these key areas.

Now that we are partnering with horses to facilitate our own much needed healing, it makes no sense to me to revert to our tired old patterns. When we are focusing on completing tasks and goals and overly engaging rational and logical parts of our minds, we avoid strengthening our more intuitive, feeling-based way of living. Or our more horse-like and feminine way of being. It is for these reasons that I passionately recommend using more reflective based sessions and also some purely observational sessions, rather than always suggesting tasks, activities or goals for clients.

Instead, encourage your clients to drop more deeply into their relationship with themselves through regular practice of body-based work and continually accessing the flow of their emotions. Allow client and horse time to just *be together*; allow time to simply observe a herd of horses. Even with corporate clients this is possible and, I would argue, preferable, by showing them a more energy-conserving way of being; how to minimize stress levels; how to be in the relationship *at all times* and how to support their herd (team), rather than constantly leading or pushing their team solely in pursuit of goals.

I co-led an innovative workshop recently which was purely observational as we were working with feral herds of ponies in the New Forest National Park in Hampshire, UK. No touching or physical interaction was allowed as this protects the horses from too much human interaction, as well as maintaining participants' safety. Instead, we watched and spent time with the ponies in their environment and on their terms. What was fascinating, though, was that over the period of just a few hours and from being mere observers, different herds seemed to accept us into a mutually shared space. From the beginning of the day, where we sat watching our first herd who stayed close by grazing contentedly, to the middle of the day where a couple of curious stallions approached us, right through to the end of the day where our human group walked as part of a dual-species herd, seemingly accepted into a large and diverse herd of ponies and donkeys. I believe this happened relatively quickly because of our approach; we were self-focused, body-focused, energy-focused, non-goal focused, open, curious and mindful. We worked on shifting and keeping our energy levels down. We respected the herd's collective boundaries. We did not approach them and, perhaps most significantly, we did not ask anything of them.

The benefits and learning for myself and the participants were significant. We all came away with a whole new frame of reference for understanding ourselves and all horses better. This resulted from simply *being* with horses on *their* terms and in *their* environment, rather than doing something structured with them on *our* terms and in *our* environment. The potential outcomes seemed to increase in variety and depth. Through solely observing herds of horses in a more natural environment, it seems that we can learn lessons in leadership, team management, relationship, energy awareness, focus, body awareness, environmental awareness and flexibility, to name just a few.

In equine facilitated work, the more we can help our clients, whatever their role in life, to become more in touch with themselves, including their bodies, emotions and relationship approaches, then the more we are helping the horses to do their job. As well as facilitating *real* change in our clients, as the last thing most of them need is further goals to achieve. In this regard then we are also contributing to a much needed shift in wider society away from a predominantly thinking and doing-based approach to life.

I am certain that horses prefer being with us when we are self-reflective and our priority is on *being* rather than *doing*. With much practice, guidance and self-awareness, it is possible to shift to a level of being able to achieve tasks with horses *while* maintaining a strong connection to one's self, body, emotions, energy and thoughts. However, *if* we bypass the learning and practice involved in doing this, we are simply reverting to our present default positions of doing, talking and thinking our way through life. Consequently, we will not get the best out of the horses we work with, nor will they really enjoy working with us. Further, our clients will not be encouraged to shift out of their long-standing habits caused through a mind-body split and resulting in avoidance, dissociation and incongruence.

Time and time again, I watched the horses shift in their desire to connect with a client when the client paid full attention to their body, acknowledged a true feeling, or simply allowed themselves to enjoy being with the horse rather than *doing* something. The evidence was incontrovertible: Horses prefer reflective rather than active interactions with us. This is not to say though they don't also enjoy having fun with us whether on the ground or riding as some of them clearly seem to. However, for the vast majority of the time horses seem to languidly enjoy being, rather than doing. And for me, this is one of their biggest gifts to us as a species that we can receive and embody.

It is my sense though that in some areas of equine facilitated practice, the emphasis is still very much on carrying out tasks. I find this hard to understand, as the horses are very clear on this. Being just ourselves, we are repeatedly told by our society, is not enough; we need to be doing *something*. However, the horses tell us the very opposite: That being ourselves is more than enough; in fact, it is plenty. After all, that is how they go through life and rather happily I might add, too.

Here are some general suggestions for balancing session content in this regard; for encouraging clients to get out of their head and into their body, as well as strengthening the right-brain while giving the left-brain a rest:

1. Strike a healthy balance between active, reflective and observational sessions.
2. Use fewer problem solving exercises that require a substantially cognitive approach.
3. Emphasize the connection to the body.
4. Emphasize the role of emotions and allow space for the client to feel their emotions.
5. Reduce the amount of time spent on cognitive-based activities such as lectures, presentations, handouts and classroom-based exercises, or learning new models and systems.
6. Reduce the amount of time spent talking. As a facilitator, you can lead on this by planning some silent times and activities. In doing so, however, it is vital that you and all your staff also model this, as it sets the tone and helps people feel reassured. It is surprising how uncomfortable many people are with being asked to remain silent. You can also model, when you do speak, how to do so by speaking from your heart and

your core and not just your head and your throat. Clients are then helped to engage with themselves and others in a more powerfully authentic, connected and grounded way.

Through employing a good balance of observational, reflective and active methods therefore, we and our clients can truly begin to embody 'The Way of The Horse', and contribute to a much needed shift in wider society in the process too.

Questioning Techniques

Another area I feel is very important in our work is developing an effective questioning technique. What I have experienced is that when the facilitator does *not* overly intervene and ask too many questions, and in particular avoids using direct or intrusive questions, then the best conditions are set for learning and healing to take place.

I find that asking one or two open questions of a client is often a good approach, and I also ensure it is coming from a place of *feeling and intuition* rather than purely my mind. I then let the client find their own way to their answers rather than suggesting possible answers. An example of a helpful question I often use is: *'How was that for you?'*

Then... and this is really important and, I think, where practitioners can fall down, try to refrain from asking too many further, probing questions. By asking that initial feeling-based and open, general question you have given the client space and time, allowing them to come to their answers in their own time. You have done enough to bring them to a place of increased awareness in that moment. When we keep asking further questions, maybe in an eagerness to fix our clients, to prove we 'know our stuff', and/or how good we are, we are impacting the *quality* of the awareness that has just gently filtered up into the client's consciousness. We are then at risk of imposing *our* agenda onto them. We are asking them to follow our agenda and really *meet our needs* in that moment, rather than stay with where the client is at. The session then becomes about meeting the practitioner's needs and not enabling the best possible experience for the client.

Also, by interjecting our own ideas too soon, or even at all, we can actually halt the gentle process going on both *within* the client and *between* the client and the horse. We can actually arrest the individual's growth or the relationship that is building between horse and person by doing so. It really is vital that we do not fall into this trap to satisfy our professional persona more than our client's development.

I also try to avoid using potentially leading questions which contain any kind of presumption on my part, and instead allow clients to make their own interpretations of what they experience. By carefully using very soft and expansive questions through the use of '*how*', we give our clients maximum space to speak their truth. Asking leading, closed or directive questions can potentially place your interpretation into the client's mind. This is best avoided as much as possible and is the hallmark of respecting their boundaries and pace of growth.

It is easy to get caught up in the habit of thinking we need to ask more questions and that if we don't, we are not good enough, somehow. However, I know that when I have been in the position of participant or client, I have personally experienced this as sometimes being too intrusive. Trusting the pace of the client's process, therefore, and the horse's guidance is key to allowing things to unfold. Again, it takes time and practice to hone this skill, as well as the willingness to allow the horse to take the lead at times.

Staying *with* and *in* the questions can be an important part of our clients' experience. Giving them space and time to find their own answers in their own time is a crucial part of their healing process. If we remember this at all times and give our horses space to guide, we are well on our way towards supporting people to the best of our abilities.

Part II

Industry Wide Issues

Quality must prevail over quantity, with a close eye kept on the impact on the horses at all times; we must not heal one species at the expense of another.

Over the past few years the popularity and recognition of equine facilitated practice has flourished across the world. In the UK alone, I would estimate that from a starting place of about twenty professionals fifteen years ago, there are now several hundred practitioners, innumerable organizations, businesses and training providers, and a varying range of methodologies and client bases.

On the one hand this is very positive, as it means the increased recognition of the benefits of working in this way with horses. As well as an increase in service provision for a wide range of people. It is important to also acknowledge that there is a lot of very good practice being carried out by conscientious, thoughtful and well-trained practitioners all around the world today. This clearly needs to be recognized, celebrated and further encouraged.

On the other hand, such rapid growth has inevitably meant that the development of common standards and regulation for this rapidly growing industry has lagged far behind. This situation has also led to concerns about the quality of some of the current practices and training. My aim here is to raise some of these issues for discussion.

In terms of ethical practice, it seems that the main training organizations do, for the most part, each have a code of ethics, but the ability to keep a check on people post-qualification and redress any ethical concerns is patchy. Some organizations are trying to do so, but an increasing number of people are being trained and certified to partner with horses to support vulnerable clients, without any form of ongoing monitoring being in place.

Further, it remains the case that without overall regulation, people in associated professional areas are currently able to offer equine facilitated services without having taken any formal equine facilitated training. There still remains a perception, unfortunately, that it is possible to deliver equine facilitated services through simply combining one's current profession, such as being a qualified therapist, with a love of horses. As a result, one can still come across well-meaning but unqualified people offering some form of this work. This usually happens as an addition to already existing equine, coaching, holistic health or therapeutic businesses. For example, horse trainers, equestrian coaches, therapeutic riding centers, leadership coaches, natural horsemanship centers, animal healers or alternative health professionals have all been attracted to this method and begun offering this work to varying degrees. All of which is perhaps inevitable in any newly emerging innovative method and parallels can be found in other professions which have emerged in recent decades such as alternative health therapies and life coaching.

For many of us, these issues are of great concern and our industry clearly needs to start addressing them to improve the validity and quality of this work. As emphasized throughout, equine-partnered work is a highly specialized form of intervention requiring a very specific set of skills, knowledge and experience. Further still, it brings together two areas of professional expertise and so practitioners need to be skilled in both aspects. The ability to work with people on their challenges in life is one important part of the equation of this work, balanced by strong but sensitive equine experience. If the balance is tipped more one way than the other, this intervention can fall short of its true potential.

One of the fundamental areas which directly impacts on this profession is the scope and quality of current practitioner training on offer. I have great concerns about the present trend in offering very short and inexpensive courses, sometimes as short as three or four days, which in some cases can result in practitioners being 'fully qualified' to offer equine facilitated programs. In addition, I have concerns about the lack of focus in some programs on both the role and well-being of the horses and the personal development of trainees, which are vital and integral elements of delivering this method well.

It is also presently the case that Equine Facilitated Learning (EFL) in particular, is a very permeable area of professional practice to enter, with a wide range of people and levels of experience being accepted by training providers. This may mean that clients and horses could be left lacking support if unsuitably experienced professionals are being trained. It could also be that this 'open-door policy' is likely to be unsustainable in the long-term if the market becomes saturated, and quality most certainly risks being diluted.

Both the public and the profession need to be able to identify who are the correctly trained and insured professionals operating, otherwise the credibility of the entire industry is potentially weakened. Similarly, potential funding bodies and statutory service providers who assess applications for this intervention are unlikely to know, for example, who the credible certifying organizations are, or the differences between the present equine facilitated services and approaches on offer. Therefore, as an industry we need to make these definitions and parameters clear, transparent and applied across the board, in order to promote the field as consistent and legitimate.

It is also apparent to me and others that while the profession is still undergoing an enthusiastic phase of growth, one less positive side effect of this is that there is presently something of an uncomfortable 'culture of fear' within the industry. Perhaps this is concerning needing to 'stick together' as a new and emerging field? Or, of feeling unsafe about criticizing the practices of our peers for fear of being ostracized in a small arena? Whatever the reasons, there is fear of speaking out about practices that do not feel right; concerns about quality and depth of some of the training on offer, and an objective assessment about the impact on the horses. Many friends and colleagues speak privately about their concerns, yet dare not publicly raise them. The irony of this situation is that we look to the horses to learn how to feel and express our emotions more fluidly and develop emotional congruency, but cannot yet bring ourselves to do this effectively among our peers. Further, paradoxically, while we are learning to be more emotionally intelligent, there are some methods being used which potentially inhibit the horses from freely expressing *their* feelings, needs and preferences.

A further concern I have is that some approaches to equine facilitated practice seem to involve little more than a series of tasks or activities. While I recognize that there can be some benefits for certain client groups to completing task-based exercises, I would argue that it is still important to maintain a mindful approach to the use of the horses throughout. This is so that we can attend to what their feedback is telling us about how the horse is feeling, how the client is progressing, and also what is happening in the *relationship* between client and horse.

As some recent research undertaken at an addiction treatment facility in Norway demonstrates, the relationship between the client and the horse is crucial: *'All except one of the participants (P6, who had participated in only one HAT session) emphasized that their relationship with one or more of the horses was one of the most important characteristics of HAT* [Horse Assisted Therapy].'[9]

In terms of research into equine facilitated practice, there is currently a great deal of evidence being gathered about the many benefits to the wide range of clients able to access these services. However, very little research is presently being focused on the impact on the horses involved, or indeed coming directly from the clients themselves. At the time of writing this book I have come across just two studies into the effect on the horses' physical and emotional well-being in equine facilitated programs.[10]

One reason for this present disparity may be the inevitable side effect of the enthusiasm driving the need for empirical data to prove the efficacy and scope of this work. I also sense, however, that overlooking the real impact on the horses involved means that we can carry on growing without having to make fundamental changes to our practice, or take the time to *really* train and embody these skills. However, I am hopeful that as our awareness grows, this imbalance will begin to be addressed.

Finally, as discussed throughout, our own ongoing self-improvement is vital in this work. This is an area that I believe is currently paid insufficient attention in some equine facilitated training programs and models, yet it is something that is essential to being a good practitioner. There is a general expectation that any therapist, counselor or coach we may employ will have undertaken a recognized professional training, done sufficient personal development work on themselves and be adhering to strict professional standards and codes of ethics within their practice. My view is that we must not expect our equine facilitated clients to accept anything less than this from us either, as we carefully take their support into our hands.

In this second part of the book, I am going to focus on some of these areas in more depth. Specifically on the areas of training; the issues of terminology and practice boundaries; the line between Equine Facilitated Learning, Equine Facilitated Psychotherapy and Equine Facilitated Therapy, and the use of horsemanship approaches in equine facilitated practice. Concluding with a look at the fundamentals of caring for our horses in the context of delivering our work.

Chapter 11

TERMINOLOGY, PRACTICE BOUNDARIES AND TRAINING

One of the difficulties in this industry at present is the confusing array of terms, acronyms and definitions regarding the various types of equine facilitated practice. Practitioners and training providers around the world are all using a variety of terms, some of which can appear potentially confusing to both the public and those wishing to enter this field professionally. Therefore, the terminology currently being used, plus training program remits, clearly need tightening up to help the field move forward. This is perhaps a further inevitable outcome of such a rapidly evolving profession, but given the size of the industry now, I feel, as training providers and practitioners, we need to be crystal clear about the terms we use, as well as ensuring that our remit is clearly defined and made public.

In this presently unregulated field, on undertaking an Internet search nowadays, it is not uncommon to see any one of the following scenarios which I personally find unclear: a psychotherapist, counselor or therapist also offering 'Equine Facilitated Psychotherapy' as one of their professional services on their website, even though they have not completed any equine facilitated training; someone qualified in either Equine Facilitated Learning (EFL) or Equine Assisted Learning (EAL) using the term 'therapy' on their website and in their marketing materials generally; or someone who offers a range of therapies, including equine facilitated ones, but who is not a qualified psychotherapist, yet they are using the term 'Equine Facilitated Psychotherapy' (EFP) on their website. It is frustrating when one comes across such cases; I can only imagine how this looks to the general public or referral agencies...

The next issue specifically concerns the therapy-branch of

this work. However, as I am not a therapist or psychotherapist, I am only going to touch upon it here. One of the most pressing but challenging areas in this regard, I feel, is that concerning the differentiation between 'Equine Facilitated/Assisted Psychotherapy' (EFP/EAP) and 'Equine Facilitated/Assisted Therapy' (EFT/EAT). It is not uncommon to see both EFP or EAT in particular being used as a catch-all for any therapy-based equine facilitated services and training programs. To compound this even further, 'therapy' can also, of course, include therapeutic riding and hippotherapy. Yet my own understanding, and from speaking at length to my EFP colleagues, is that 'therapy' and 'psychotherapy' can be very different things and have very different requirements in terms of duration of training, personal development and investment. This issue clearly needs further research and clarification to help the industry move forward productively.

An additional complicating factor with regard to therapy, is that each country differs in respect to training in psychotherapy and other forms of therapy, so it is vital to check the regional differences as many equine facilitated training providers train people from outside their country. For example, many equine facilitated training providers are in the United States, yet their criteria differs greatly to that of the UK in terms of qualification and accreditation requirements specifically in mental health, counseling and psychotherapy.

Another common area of overlap happens when people use the generic term 'Equine Therapy' as a way to describe what they do. In the early days this short-hand description enabled many of us to explain to the general public what this work was about, as it was such a new and innovative method to describe effectively. However, now that the field has expanded and there are so many more training and service providers, it is clearly much more important to use precise terminology as well as clearly define our practice boundaries. Further, it is imperative that referring agencies of vulnerable client groups, such as statutory providers, health services and mental health services, all know exactly what is being offered and what the credentials of the professionals involved are. In addition, any lack of clarity in definition and remit can also potentially confuse providers of funding for equine facilitated services, where the risk is that funding could potentially be granted to unsuitably qualified and trained professionals. Neither of which benefit potential clients or the industry as a whole.

A Way Forward:
Suggestions for Improved Clarity, Simplicity and Quality

In light of just some of these complexities that I have outlined, I would therefore like to recommend some simplification of terminology and good practice suggestions for moving forward from this point.

Training providers: Clarifying the language and terminology you use to most accurately reflect the precise forms of equine facilitated practices you are offering training in. Also, only accepting onto your equine facilitated programs those who fully meet the minimum standards in terms of qualifications and experience.

Practitioners: Working within your professional areas of competence and to your code of ethics and standards as produced by your equine facilitated qualifying body, and/or mental health qualifying body, where relevant. So, if you are trained in Equine Facilitated/Assisted *Learning* (or Coaching), then I suggest you can only offer *learning-based* services and steer clear of the word 'therapy' altogether in *all* of your marketing and literature. If you are a fully qualified psychotherapist (in whatever approach of psychotherapy you are trained in) and licensed and accredited to practice, then if you have *also* undertaken a suitable equine facilitated training, you can then offer Equine Facilitated/Assisted *Psychotherapy* (EFP/EAP). If you hold any other type of mental health qualification but are not a qualified psychotherapist, and you have undertaken a suitable equine facilitated training, then you can only deliver Equine Facilitated/ Assisted *Therapy* (EFT/EAT), and refrain from using the terms 'Psychotherapy' or 'EFP/EAP'.

Trainees: For those interested in entering this profession, I recommend carefully researching the many training options available; speaking to the different training providers and seeking to apply to the most relevant Equine Facilitated Learning, Equine Facilitated Psychotherapy or Equine Facilitated Therapy training programs which matches their specific qualifications, background and areas of experience.

Further Issues Concerning Training

Training of equine facilitated professionals is the starting point for the majority of people entering the field and therefore a key contributing element towards the quality, integrity and efficacy of this work, as well as the overall industry's standards.

In terms of the horses' role and well-being, it is of course, the training providers who model how the horses are involved and to what degree the horses are allowed freedom, autonomy, choice and responsibility. Many trainees and newly qualified practitioners will inevitably use their trainers' methods as their baseline, whether for good or bad. Therefore training providers hold a high degree of responsibility in these key areas.

One psychologist I spoke to who had completed an initial equine facilitated training course, gave me her account of how she experienced this. As well as highlighting the apparently limited role of the horses being used, seemingly in order purely to complete tasks, this account also raises a number of other concerns around current practice and training trends. One is the issue of participants being asked to focus mainly on undertaking activities at the expense of developing a relationship between themselves and the horses. Another is the question of how robust or not current training providers are at selecting the most suitably qualified people, particularly with regard to equine facilitated therapy and psychotherapy.

'I did the training in 2010 while I was doing my clinical training in psychology. Overall I felt disappointed at the end of the training. I finished the training feeling quite confused about EAP. Specifically, the model was explained well and we practiced many of the activities and exercises of the model. However, I felt it was only that: Practicing some tasks and activities without an adequate explanation or reflection on the purpose of it or how you then process the feelings that emerge. I basically could not understand how you call this 'therapy.'

Being around horses is powerful and therapeutic; that's something I have experienced myself. But to call something 'psychotherapy' requires other elements as well, such as processing feelings and thoughts, containment, etc.

In this training I felt the focus was only to do a task and complete it without much time or reflection on the process and without considering the role of the horse! It seemed that you only used the horse to achieve the task, rather than focusing on the interaction with the horse.

I am aware I might sound overcritical but I wanted to say that, regardless of my disappointing experience, I would do the training again in order to be open and give it another go. It might have been down to different factors why the training did not feel satisfying; for example, the facilitators or the team. Something else I have been wondering about is what we mean by 'mental health practitioner'? Mental health practitioners do not always have therapy training, so I remember that in the training there were only three out of twelve participants, including myself, that had trained or were in training as psychotherapists or psychologists.'

As regards the quality and depth of training, my overall

feeling is that many of the training courses presently on offer are considerably too short, sometimes as brief as just three or four days. I do not believe it is at all possible to fully grasp the potential of this method, or do any reflective professional practice or substantial personal work in this amount of time. In my opinion, this is merely an introduction to this work and not a serious or sufficiently rigorous training program.

Also, I feel that such a short training process is usually far too condensed. It takes time to learn and integrate new skills. It takes time to illicit change in our thought patterns and behavior, for example, new neural pathways take time to create and strengthen. Further still, one's own personal journey of growth and integration requires time, this is why some equine facilitated programs such as the Eponaquest® Apprenticeship are a year long. I passionately believe that a gestation period of integration and personal growth is needed before stepping out as a professional offering a service to others.

A further concern I have is around the issue of accountability, both concerning the training providers themselves but also their certified practitioners. As many more training providers emerge around the world, we need to ask, what, if any, checks and balances are currently in place to monitor the quality of what they are offering. One solution which some training providers are now adopting is to work towards formal accreditation. While there are clear benefits to this approach, it is imperative for me that meeting the accrediting body's requirements does not detract from or negatively impact on the natural process of the horse's role, which is at the heart of this work. In addition, each training provider needs to have a clear system in place for monitoring certified practitioners post-qualification to ensure they remain 'fit for practice' and that they are engaging in supervision and ethical practices, as well as providing continuing professional development opportunities.

Another hugely important consideration is the selection of trainees. If we compare the industry to one of its closest neighbors which is that of counseling and psychotherapy, applicants to these training courses have to demonstrate suitability for the profession. If they do not, for example, show sufficient self-awareness, aptitude for growth or a strong ability to empathize, it is highly unlikely that they will be accepted onto such courses. Therefore, given the strong therapeutic potential inherent in equine facilitated interventions, I feel it would be helpful to be applying similar parameters in this field.

What follows are some of the key considerations that I feel are helpful when selecting trainees. These can also serve as a guide for those interested in undertaking training to help them select the most appropriate training provider for them.

Selecting Trainees

I believe that people interested in entering this profession need to be naturally empathetic and intuitive; able to hold a safe, reflective space or container for others; have good inter-personal boundaries and be mentally and emotionally balanced, with a strong connection to their own body. In addition, it is important that they are not deeply laden with their own wounds and in such need of considerable healing themselves first, for example people with active PTSD, severe depression or non-recovered abuse or addictions. Obviously this varies from individual to individual. For some people with sufficient support from a therapist, undertaking such a training may be possible. Of course, being mindful of the impact on the group as a whole is vital in these cases, too.

I also believe it is essential that an applicant demonstrates a substantial commitment towards their own personal development, before, during and post-qualification. I am not referring here to continuing professional development (which needs to take place as well), but rather their own ongoing *personal healing and growth*.

Another essential part of this personal development in respect of this work is that trainees have experienced the healing and learning potential of equine facilitated practice themselves first as a participant. This work cannot be learned intellectually through books and definitely not through taking online courses. It can only be felt and experienced in your body and outside in the horse's presence and environment. It is vital, in my view, that facilitators know exactly how it feels to be vulnerable in the presence of horses and other people, and how the horses can help us shift and grow. I would also advise people to experience a variety of the different approaches and models that currently exist, so that they find the one that most resonates with them personally, and that also offers the best training and approach for the area of the work and clients that they are drawn to.

For Equine Facilitated Learning, although generally no formal qualifications are presently required, I have found that experience and pre-qualifications in the following areas can be helpful: Coaching, education, basic counseling, teaching, youth and community work, caring professionals, support work, some somatic-based body work, business coaches and riding instructors/coaches.

Experience with Horses is Vital

In addition to the above considerations, it goes without saying that substantial experience with horses is an inherent prerequisite and aspect of this work. Therefore, reiterating this crucial element, I hope, will be helpful and I would urge training providers to keep this at the forefront of their minds when selecting trainees. It is vital that this element is not overlooked or diluted by training providers as it is a fundamental requirement to working alongside horses.

Where we are partnering with another species, in this case horses, to offer a professional service to the public, this requires practitioners to have substantial experience and understanding of horses. Preferably also with a commitment to developing a non-dominant approach to horse-handling and relationships with horses. I am very firmly of the belief that this is true regardless of which equine facilitated approach is being used, including those models which employ a team approach of a therapist/coach and equine specialist. In my view, everyone involved in delivering *any* aspect of this work must have substantial experience and knowledge of horses. Given the subtle nature of this work, practitioners need to have an intimate understanding of and strong connection with horses. The most effective way to gain this is by spending as much time as possible observing herds of horses and through obtaining experience of handling them. Ultimately of course, the best way to do this is through owning your own horse, as these day-to-day interactions provide the very best opportunity for building such intimate understanding and hands-on experience of handling, caring for, training and exercising horses. However, I understand that not everyone can afford to keep a horse, so finding alternative ways to regularly engage with horses is vital if you wish to do this type of work.

To begin to understand the horse's responses to clients and ourselves, as well as other horses; to gain a good grasp of the many variations of equine behaviors, subtle and obvious body language, herd dynamics, equine needs, and vastly complex areas of emotional and energetic communication among horses and between horses and people, can only come from extensive time in the field; literally with a herd.

Chapter 12

The Line Between Equine Facilitated Learning and Equine Facilitated Psychotherapy/Therapy

The difference between Equine Facilitated Learning (EFL) and either Equine Facilitated Psychotherapy (EFP) or Equine Facilitated Therapy (EFT) is one aspect of this work which is particularly confusing both for practitioners and for potential clients seeking to access these services. This line can be quite hard to distinguish and can easily be overstepped by inexperienced or well-intentioned but insufficiently skilled or supervised practitioners.

To a certain extent this is a matter of agreeing a standardized terminology for this developing field of work, as discussed in the previous chapter. However, it is also indicative of a wider problem which I believe needs addressing. In particular, if EFL practitioners who are not suitably qualified begin to deliver EFP or EFT then that is something which would cause me considerable concern. This is especially true if they are working with vulnerable client groups such as those suffering from trauma. Conversely, if a practitioner advertises as offering therapy or psychotherapy but in fact purely offers EFL, then clients expecting to receive therapy could indeed feel upset. To complicate things further, the very nature of our work with horses is often therapeutic. Yet even when pure EFL work is being undertaken, the clients' past issues will often arise and of course in that situation, we still need to have the skills to deal with and contain these issues, more on this particular aspect in a minute.

Ella Jones, Director of LEAP in the UK, describes the general difference between EFP and EFL thus: *'In EFP you are looking back to the client's past as well as the present and future. In EFL, you are focusing much more in the present and towards the future.'* I usually describe my EFL work as being personal development oriented, aimed at changing patterns of behavior and learning new tools and life skills. Whereas Equine Facilitated Psychotherapy or Equine Facilitated Therapy incorporates more deeply focused work, often involving working through childhood issues, and/or addressing specific conditions through targeted, therapeutic methods and approaches.

A basic rule of thumb which I would like to suggest, that I feel is clear and helpful, is that if you are not a qualified mental health professional, therapist, counselor or psychotherapist, then you can only train in and deliver Equine Facilitated Learning. If you wish to also offer Equine Facilitated Psychotherapy or Equine Facilitated Therapy to your clients, then you need to team up with a suitably qualified equine facilitated psychotherapist or therapist.

In the rest of this chapter I am going to concentrate on how to deal with any therapeutic issues that arise in EFL specifically.

Therapeutic Issues in Equine Facilitated Learning

In my own work I always make it very clear that my practice is purely Equine Facilitated Learning. I describe it as personal development with a particular focus on issues such as developing healthier relationships, learning to set and respect boundaries, healing the mind-body split and developing emotional agility. I also state that it is not suitable for those with 'active mental health issues without the consent of their therapist.'

In essence, EFL works in a similar way to life coaching. However, as mentioned above, one of the complexities of horse-involved work is that it is also inherently therapeutic in nature. Whoever your client is, inevitably something from their history and childhood can be triggered through being around horses as they can very quickly evoke the emotions of fear and vulnerability in a lot of people. Further, our clients are inherently entering a setting where vulnerability is allowed and encouraged to surface. It is therefore beholden on the EFL practitioner to be skilled enough to manage the times when memories or traumas surface, and to keep the client safe through re-focusing them to the present moment.

In addition, because this work is so powerful, practitioners themselves can be 'triggered' both by their clients and the horses, so that their own issues surface within a session. Therefore, they need to be adept at dealing with their own 'emotional disruption' while also remaining fully present for client and horses. EFL practitioners who are not sufficiently skilled to cope with some clients' issues could leave clients extremely vulnerable and exposed.

Therefore, although formal mental health qualifications are not necessary in order to carry out EFL, it is paramount that practitioners possess certain relevant skills. These include being able to empathize, having good listening skills, the ability to hold a therapeutic space, a strong desire to support people and a commitment to developing your own self-awareness. It is obviously also essential to have an understanding of the projection and transference that surfaces in any self-improvement work. This awareness can only come from undertaking one's own personal development.

As just described, as an EFL provider, one needs to be adept at helping clients re-focus on the present moment and not get lost in them telling you their story, which of course is where the horses are so helpful. This is not to say, though, that you bypass or intrude upon the client's process, as in that moment they may be accessing some very important feelings that have been deeply buried. One needs to sensitively and empathetically reflect back the client's feelings and words but also remind them that this is not a therapy session. Maybe suggest if the feelings are connected to something significant in their past, that they now seek a therapist to help them come to terms with what has arisen. Then gently re-focus their attention back to the present moment.

Going back to the horse's behavior and (if appropriate,) their own body, are very effective ways of doing this. It could also be beneficial to offer helpful suggestions for moving forward from that point, maybe through some further connection or gentle activity with the horse, such as reflective grooming. It is a very delicate balancing act of not dismissing powerful emotions and memories, while not letting the session turn into an in-depth process which you are perhaps not adept, skilled or paid to facilitate.

Therefore, it is crucial to be very clear and honest with yourself as to your capabilities and the areas you can and cannot work in. It seems increasingly common practice in this field to see on practitioners' websites a very wide range of groups of clients that they work with. This often causes me some concern around people possibly working outside of their areas of competency.

To re-cap, I feel, to work ethically we all ought to ensure we avoid offering services to client groups that we have no specific experience of working with. Knowing where our professional and competency boundaries are and sticking to them is vital. As is being very clear on all of our marketing to the public about what exactly we offer and which sorts of clients we are experienced in working with. Making this very clear at the public face of our work, particularly on our websites, is critical so that clients can access the most appropriate professional to help them and the public can have confidence in this work generally. Steer clear of referring to what you do under the generic term of 'equine assisted therapy' as a catch-all, which very often happens, if in fact you only offer EFL. In fact, it makes sense to avoid use of the term 'therapy' altogether if you are an EFL practitioner; this keeps things simpler for all concerned, not least of all the public. Make it crystal clear and tell people when they contact you whether they have found the right type of intervention or not.

Practical Suggestions for Maintaining the Boundary

As mentioned, horses can home in on underlying issues in people very quickly and sometimes within the very first session. So the professional needs to be ready for this by first finding out the client's history and current presenting issues. This can be done through asking clients to complete a comprehensive booking form. Asking these questions and also following up with a telephone call is worthwhile. In my experience, speaking to someone on the phone can often reveal much more than their written answers.

If, during this pre-booking stage, the EFL practitioner feels that the client really needs to see a therapist, then they must say this and then refer the client to someone they feel comfortable referring to, preferably someone whose work they know personally. It is tempting to always say yes, due to an urge to help, to do your work and also earn money. However, where the client's well-being is at stake, ethical good practice demands that you can be humble enough to say that you are not the best person to help this client and refer them on.

It is also very much the case that, even when you have undergone a thorough pre-booking screening of your client, deeper issues can arise in the first session. At that point, again you need to stop and reassess your client's needs, and then discuss with them whether they proceed with you, with a therapist, or both.

In my booking form, which I use for all clients whether one-to-one or group sessions, I ask whether the client is presently working with a therapist and if not, whether they have access to one. If they are working with a therapist, I sometimes also request that they obtain their therapist's permission to also undertake EFL sessions with me. I also have a pool of Equine Facilitated Psychotherapy or Therapy practitioners on file so that I can refer clients on when necessary.

It is generally a very good idea to offer an initial session to your clients to see if you can work together and whether you are the most appropriate practitioner to help them, or not. This is how most therapists and coaches operate. It gives you both a chance to meet and see if you can work together and if not, then be willing and ready to refer them to someone else that you feel can help the client more. Always remember that as your partners are horses, you cannot pretend in this work. Your horses will expose your lack of confidence as well as that of your clients, so you need to work clearly within your remit, rather than try to be something you are not.

If you are training or newly qualified, always seek support, supervision and guidance from your trainers and more experienced practitioners to help you navigate such issues. Many professionals with substantial experience under their belt offer equine facilitated supervision and consultancy to help you address the many practical and ethical aspects of running your equine facilitated practice. Use them and learn from them, as their wisdom and experience is extremely valuable and could save you, your clients and your horses a lot of angst and potential trouble.

Supervision with someone who knows how equine-partnered sessions can unfold, in my view, is essential whether you are delivering Equine Facilitated Psychotherapy, Equine Facilitated Therapy or Equine Facilitated Learning. Supervision offers a space to reflect on your own awareness and learning, as well as how to deal with the process between you and your clients. The transference and counter-transference that does arise can wreak havoc if left unconscious. In addition, especially in the early days of your practice, it will help you work through where your professional boundaries comfortably are. Personally, I recommend that, ideally, practitioners employ both a therapist and a supervisor for all of these reasons.

Continued self-improvement, professional scrutiny and support are vital in order to be a clear conduit for this work. If, during training or indeed, post-qualification, you are still not clear where this boundary is when you are practicing, then seek advice from a more experienced practitioner before you continue.

Chapter 13

Outcomes Versus Healing

It's not about the numbers;
it's about the quality of the healing potential.

As practitioners, if we get overly focused on outcomes, results or even job satisfaction, we can then allow our own agenda to prevail over the client's needs and process. We can then also definitely inhibit the horse's full and natural role, including potentially overlooking their feedback.

We are in danger of bringing our needs to the forefront if we are overly concerned with delivering a certain number of sessions, gathering evidence of the effectiveness of this type of intervention, or meeting funder's requirements. All of these are valid and important points to focus on some of the time, but they must not be the explicit or implicit driving force behind how we operate in our actual work. In our eagerness to prove the validity of this work in the mainstream arena, we can get lost in the pursuit of outcomes, measurements and numbers. However, the concern here is that this can easily take priority over *quality* of service for the client or impact on the horses.

It is absolutely the case in my experience with horses that when we don't overly focus on an outcome or agenda, this is when the real magic happens between horse and person. Dropping your expectation of what could happen or what you hope might happen, usually leads to significantly more unfolding. Having an inner or outer agenda running such as 'needing all my clients to show an increase in confidence or self-esteem', will create stress within yourself. As this then emanates around you through your energy field, it is of course picked up immediately by the horses, thus affecting their feedback.

It will also most definitely be felt by your clients. You may in turn exhibit performance anxiety, self-consciousness or other types of anxiety through this added layer of self-pressure, which risks hindering the entire process. Such feelings, of course, can quickly lead us to put pressure on the client or the horses to perform or achieve.

I learned early on that by letting things unfold naturally between horse and client, and allowing my horses to have choice as to which horse works with which client, then much more than I ever imagined, took place before my eyes. To this day, the horses' responses and actions never fail to amaze me when they can freely and intuitively guide things.

We can also, of course, become or already be too business focused and so outcomes in terms of profit can become the driving force behind what we do. In addition, currently there is a trend to market this work as much as possible, particularly on the Internet and through Social Media platforms. As a result, I am concerned that boundaries and confidentiality may potentially be being breached, as practitioners show photos and video clips of clients, sometimes also naming their clients and even describing what took place in a session, in order to prove the efficacy of this work.

We really need to be asking ourselves the following questions if we wish to regard this as a serious profession: Is this appropriate? Is this ethical? Does this maintain confidentiality and working relationship boundaries? Even with our clients' consent, the very act of using a client's story or image to promote what we do *is* questionable, in my view. I always ask myself how I would feel if I were the client in this situation, say if a therapist I was working with asked me if they could include me in their marketing. I think I have to conclude that I would be incredibly uncomfortable about it and probably decline unless it were kept completely anonymous, which of course a video cannot be.

My own experience of delivering sessions is that any form of observing, including photography – and certainly filming – is quite intrusive and is actually disruptive to the client's delicate process. Many clients need complete privacy and to feel safe, so that they can begin to access their emotions and blockages, and many clients also really do not like being observed. Even being watched by a single facilitator can be hard for some people, so self-conscious are they about feeling their emotions, accessing traumatic memories and behaving authentically, perhaps for the first time.

That so many more potential clients are being reached is, of course, a very positive development and indeed one to be celebrated. I know, wholeheartedly, the healing potential of being with horses. However, at all times, we need to keep a close eye on: What is the *quality* of work which is presently being delivered? How *rigorous* are the current training standards? What are the *impacts* on these horses? And what *safeguards* are in place to ensure our clients receive the very best when they pay us to support them?

I hope that this field does not also get further sucked down into the obsession in our logic and externally-oriented society, where outcomes and measurements prevail at the expense of the sensitive, deep healing potential that exists when a horse and a person come together in a soulful meeting. I can't help but conjure up Jung's phrase when I reflect on such experiences I have witnessed many times over between horses and clients, that, '...the meeting of two personalities is like the contact of two chemical substances; if there is any reaction, both are transformed.' Equine facilitated practice certainly has the potential to create transformations in each person who undertakes it, and often for the horses too. Therefore, by keeping our eye on the *quality* of what we offer and the fundamental *empowered role* of the horses, rather than the quantity or the boxes that need ticking, then we can step into this potential and contribute to a more conscious society, one client at a time.

In equine facilitated practice there are no quick fixes. Nothing can be taught, felt or healed in a specified period of time. It takes as long as it takes for each person. Common practice nowadays is to offer a set number of sessions to clients, for example, six to eight sessions, sometimes within a framework of what can or must be covered, and often including set tasks or exercises to take the client through.

None of the more sensitive and subtle skills the horses encourage us to develop can be taught in a set number of sessions. Horses and indeed people's impetus to change, or moreover the soul's pursuit of growth, does not respond well to prescriptive, time restricted experiences. This is incidentally why I also dislike the common practice nowadays outside of equine facilitated work, of offering a client who needs counseling or therapy, a block of six sessions of Cognitive Behavioral Therapy (CBT). Based on the spurious claim that a short burst of CBT is sufficient, when the real reason is that it is much quicker and therefore also less expensive to provide than long-term psychotherapy. But at what cost to the client's *real* and more deep-seated needs, I wonder?

Working in this limited way, with a set number or block of sessions, raises a number of further concerns. It could lead to not getting to the crux of an issue for someone sufficiently, due to lack of time. It could be possible to overload the client with too much information too quickly, and it also runs the risk of rushed sessions, in order to fit as much as possible into a time-limited period.

Funding needs to be mentioned here as it is often granted on this basis, involving a set number of sessions and usually with a desired set of outcomes to be met. However, if we start shaping our clients' and our horses' experiences to meet the requirement of current funding trends, we are on a very slippery slope indeed. A slope that could lead to support of a rather poorer quality than is actually possible with horses. This type of approach does indeed push us along the track of the horses being tools, rather than letting the organic, slower pace of the individual's mind, body and soul connect with another, in this case the horse, and let things unfold in their natural way.

If we are going to seek external funding and client referrals, which many in this field now do, then we also need to learn to be expert at obtaining funding *without* letting it shape how we actually work with the horses to support people. The key to doing this is to keep coming back to what the horses might see as beneficial. To them, a client finally able to connect to their breath and heart's desire is a 'result' in equine terms. Learning how to translate this 'outcome' into language that funding bodies or service providers require is an art all in itself. And remember, your main aim is to honor your horses and help your clients' progress, not tick boxes.

Chapter 14

HORSEMANSHIP APPROACHES WITHIN
EQUINE FACILITATED PRACTICE

SOME SUGGESTIONS, A FEW WORDS OF CAUTION
AND SOME CLARIFICATION

It is common practice in equine facilitated work to include the use of both traditional and natural horsemanship techniques and approaches. One of the most commonly used techniques is that of moving a loose horse around in a round pen or arena. This is sometimes referred to as 'active round pen work'; 'loose schooling'; or 'loose lunging'. In horsemanship, it is a method used to back and train horses.

In equine facilitated practice, however, it is used to develop specific skills in clients. These include increased confidence, verbal and non-verbal communication, leadership, motivation, energy modulation and establishing a connection with another sentient being. Indeed, this approach can lead to significant breakthroughs when carefully and sensitively undertaken. There is certainly the *potential* for healing to occur in the round pen with a loose horse, as described in my experience with Laramie in Chapter 4.

As emphasized throughout, in this work our focus needs to be on several key areas at once: The horse's feedback; connection to self and the horse (relationship); along with a continual commitment in each moment to developing our self-awareness. In other words, the focus is on the person learning or unlearning something, not the horse.

Therefore, where equine facilitated practice and horsemanship, including natural horsemanship differ greatly, is that in equine facilitated work it is not about changing something in the horse, it is about changing something in the person. In horsemanship, the focus is very definitely more on the horse and about changing something in them. Here then is where we come up against a major problem when incorporating or even exclusively using horsemanship as a methodology in equine facilitated practice. Further still, as I will seek to show, many horsemanship techniques directly oppose the best conditions for healing and growth in people, and can create stress in the horses which greatly diminishes the quality of the process for all involved, not least of all the horses.

However, as many people drawn to natural horsemanship are also attracted to equine facilitated practice, there is inevitably often some overlap of the two fields. Further, there is also some very definite confusion in this profession's and the public's perception about where and how they differ. Indeed, some equine facilitated professionals combine the two and incorporate some of the techniques in their sessions. Some, for example, even refer to their entire equine facilitated approach as 'therapeutic horsemanship'.

Differing Approaches

There is currently much debate around the traditionally taught concepts of leadership in relationship with horses. This aspect is often taught as a fundamental of natural horsemanship in particular, where students are taught that they must assume the role of leader at all times. In order to achieve this goal, they must be competent and capable at physically moving the horse around, and this is particularly often demonstrated through the use of the round pen. This approach will be discussed in more depth later.

More generally, there is also a debate going on concerning the use of round pens for horses in all areas of horsemanship. Some horse professionals dislike putting horses in a confined space to move them around under any situation. They maintain that, although the horse is loose, his choice is severely limited by the size and shape of a round pen in particular, which has no corners for the horse to retreat to for some degree of safety. On the other hand, some natural horsemanship devotees and equine facilitated practitioners still regard the round pen as their first choice for a lot of their work with clients. As with so many aspects of this practice, this is another complex area.

A Sensitive and Empowering Approach to Active Round Pen

Personally, my own experiences of interacting with horses in round pens or an enclosed arena, have been very positive. At Eponaquest® and subsequently on my own and with my clients, I have found working and interacting with horses in a round pen to be both healing and hugely enjoyable. However, as I shall describe, this is because I have always undertaken this activity using a somewhat different approach to the ones commonly used in both traditional and natural horsemanship. In addition, my main priority at all times has been both the well-being of the horse and the relationship with the horse.

I therefore advocate an approach which I believe is sensitive, considered and respectful. This involves simultaneously engaging the following elements: Being congruent, with body, emotions, mind and intention in alignment; respecting the horse's personal space and boundaries; engaging the horse through your own and the horse's energetic heart-fields, and learning to transfigure control and dominance into assertive but sensitive leadership. I have found that this approach can lead to developing a much softer relationship with horses. One which is generally also much calmer and the horses seem to really enjoy.

So, How Do You Do This?

As trainees and participants at Eponaquest®, we regularly practiced sensing our own and others' energy fields, that invisible yet physically tangible field of energy that emanates from our body and out into the collective, affecting everyone in our vicinity. Once we were fluid in this non-verbal form of communication with the horses, we then got to take it into a more active interaction, which we did in the round pen with a loose horse.

This approach incorporates establishing a heart-based connection with the horse before even entering the round pen space with her, and then approaching, using your awareness of the horse's personal boundaries and energy field.

Once a mutual relationship is established, you can walk around the area together for a while, stop, walk, trot or canter together, if safe to do so with that horse and while protecting your own boundaries. Then you begin to incorporate asking the horse to freely move around you. When you are feeling confident and fully safe, you can then move to a more advanced level and let the horse suggest direction, pace and movements; truly connected in a dance. Throughout, and this is crucial to maintaining the relationship, the person pays mutual attention to the horse's feedback at all times, and to their body, energy and breath, stopping when necessary to explore a sensation or block that has arisen, or maybe focus on their breathing.

It takes significant practice, gentle guidance and time to incorporate all of these elements into a fluid approach. It therefore absolutely cannot be taught in a single session, as these many elements and developed skills are needed to be able to do this effectively. This involves mutual respect, sensitivity, asking, suggesting, assertively leading and gentleness. Above all else, there is always a two-way and equal relationship, where both horse's and human's needs are respected. Completing the task and the need to dominate another sentient being must not be a part of the equation. In over ten years of doing it this way, I have not seen any horses exhibit stress or fear when this much softer approach is adopted.

In terms of our work though, this of course requires the practitioner to be fully fluent in this approach first, in order to be able to support their clients and their horses in sessions.

Contrast this more sensitive approach in the round pen then, to the commonly used natural horsemanship methods of sending the horse away through pressure until they submit to you and 'join-up', and we can see two very different approaches. In this latter approach, what I have frequently seen are highly stressed horses and ultimately highly submissive horses. More on the dangers of employing this approach in our practice below.

One of the other significant differences in this more sensitive approach is that minimal equipment is used. What this leads to is discovering inner resources to engage and motivate the horse. The most you need is something to act as a boundary device to maintain your personal space as the horse moves freely around you. With clients, this is an essential piece of safety equipment but nothing further is needed which leaves the horse free to move as they wish and also prevents your clients, or you, depending on pieces of equipment. This is an important distinction to make when comparing this approach to more traditional or natural forms of working with horses, which tends to be heavily equipment dependent. This means then that this approach strives to remove as many items of dominance as possible in the relationship between person and the horse.

The Natural Horsemanship Approach

I have always had difficulty with both traditional and more recently natural horsemanship approaches. The reasons for this are because

I feel they tend to focus almost exclusively on changing something about the horse. They also tend to be inherently dominance-based, still. And crucially, they avoid, to a great extent, the person's effect on the horse through not focusing on the inner process of the handler. In my experience with horses however, it is when we actually focus on our inner process which either directly attracts or repels the horses.

Natural horsemanship has become somewhat controversial in very recent years, following its peak of popularity in the past couple of decades. In terms of an approach to equestrianism, it is still a relatively new approach to working with and training horses. I refer to it as controversial because, at first glance, it purports to offer a softer way of relating to our equine friends. Some of its origins stem from observing and experimenting with wild horses and therefore many trainers claim that it is employing tactics horses use to 'naturally' relate to each other.

In my early days of exploring the field of equine facilitated practice, I inevitably encountered this parallel growth and interest in natural horsemanship. There was a general belief being portrayed by some that the two were in fact essential partners. So I began attending natural horsemanship demonstrations and taster days to find out more for myself.

My own personal experiences of natural horsemanship have involved witnessing a mixture of some impressive, smooth and seemingly soft techniques on the one hand, but on the other, a lot of gut-level suspicion and also several unpleasant experiences. In addition, some of the horses' responses I have seen have seemingly involved a lot of confusion towards these methods, particularly when in their owner's hands as they are trying to learn these techniques. Further, I have seen some horses become very sour as a result of being subjected to some of these approaches. The amount of rope waving and use of sticks and special halters that is commonly deemed necessary just adds to my distrust.

On several occasions I was left wondering: Where was the 'softness' in any of this? What was 'natural' about these experiences? Rather, they felt rough, clunky and more about control and showmanship than genuine horsemanship. I also felt a great deal of empathy for the owners of these horse, who were often left watching helplessly on the side-lines as a trainer worked with their horse. How many people reading this can relate to this experience of the all-powerful, all-knowing 'horse experts' in whose hands we place our sensitive animals?

I am now very firmly of the belief that many of these techniques are actually very far from being 'natural'. In fact I have become quite a fierce advocate *against* the use of the majority of these techniques in any horse-human relationships, but most especially in the case of equine facilitated practice. Instead, to me it feels like merely a continuation of the dominance-submission paradigm of more traditional forms of horsemanship, rather than really establishing a partnership with horses but covered up under the guise of being more 'natural'.

However, I must balance these unpleasant experiences with the fact that I know people who have explored natural horsemanship to a greater extent than I have and who have found some very helpful techniques to use with their horses. There is no doubt that some natural horsemanship techniques in the right hands can get results. Nonetheless, my personal experiences were enough to dissuade me from going down that particular road any further and as always, I come back to what the horses seem to prefer, and I can't help but conclude that less is more with them, including less pressure, force and 'training' of them.

Many of the commonly used natural horsemanship techniques for moving a horse loose in a round pen look nothing like the sensitive approach outlined earlier. As a dancer, I can easily equate the sensitive approach to being asked to dance and both partners taking a full role in the dance. There is two-way communication.

One is not *making* the other move around the dance floor with them, but each is suggesting and answering in a mutual exchange of energy, intention and emotional resonance. However, I have on many occasions been on the receiving end of a dance partner who uses ego and dominance to drag me around the dance floor, insisting I move in a certain direction, pace and style and severely limiting my say in the dance. To say the least, these are not at all satisfying or enjoyable dances. Instead, I feel like an object for that person's needs and ego. I imagine many horses feel the same when being *made* to move around the round pen, obeying every whim and desire of handlers who are unwilling to listen to their horses and unable truly to be in a partnership.

In both situations it seems to me that fear is the driving force behind this dominance. Fear of receiving feedback from another sentient being and fear of having to *really* change some habits of a lifetime to achieve the same goal but without resorting to force.

I find this hugely frustrating because when done respectfully and softly, working with horses in a round pen can be very playful and joyful, and they can also potentially be transcendent experiences. On a number of occasions, I have felt my False Self or persona completely melt away. The boundaries between me and the horse have dissolved into a tangible sense of oneness, where numinous messages and sensations filled the air. This has led me to firmly believe that when done this way, tremendous enjoyment and healing is possible in a round pen or arena with a loose horse. It does not need to involve dominance, pressure, aggression, rigid techniques, expensive tools and equipment, hours of watching professionals' DVDs, or adulation of a 'guru'. Instead, a two-way relationship is fully possible, with mutual respect, regard for one another's needs and desires, and where love and gentleness are employed.

I actually feel that where natural horsemanship went wrong, right from its very origins, was by taking its central approach from how wild horses *can* and do *sometimes* aggressively move one another about in their herds, and by misunderstanding the hierarchical structures and interplay within herds. This has turned out to be far more complex, fluid and organic than originally thought. For example, nowadays the idea of one alpha mare or stallion in all situations is being challenged. As we observe and learn more from wild herds than ever before, it turns out that these roles change and in fact are inter-changeable depending on context and survival needs. This also seems to be the case in our domesticated herds, too.

From such a starting point, many trainers employed tools like sticks and ropes to enable us, much smaller and less powerful humans, to try to move horses around in an attempt to emulate the alpha mare or stallion. But the crucial differences were that humans could never match the strength or aggression of horses on an equal footing, nor through simply adopting a controlling approach. Further, the fluidity of leadership roles within herds was not emulated between trainer and horse. Instead, a more rigid or static alpha stance was adopted and promoted to all future trainees of these methods. In addition, trainers also tried to replicate these behaviors within a confined space, the round pen, rather than on the open plains and so, in most cases, the horse could not escape the trainers' methods, no matter how dominant. Subsequently, the majority of horses submit their will and shut down their natural impulses, real power and potency, and their spirit, to meet the human's needs and desires. The key missing ingredient in all of these methods is relationship.

The Relationship with Equine Facilitated Practice

Now let's turn our attention back to where this fits in specifically with equine facilitated practice, because as I have mentioned above, unfortunately, some elements of the more dominant natural horsemanship techniques are sometimes being used in equine facilitated work, too. These may include methods which involve subjecting horses to undue pressure and stress. Even more worryingly in some cases, it appears that highly troubled clients are being shown very basic aspects of working with a loose horse in a round pen. I believe very strongly that these methods hold no enjoyment for the horses and are potentially, if not definitely, stressful for them. In my view, they are also of little benefit to our clients.

I think partly that these methods are adopted through a misguided understanding about power and control. Very often the clients who access this work have experienced profound powerlessness in their lives. Whether through trauma, abuse, addiction, or just through the trials and tribulations of surviving their childhood, many of us carry deep wounds in our psyches involving debilitating feelings of powerlessness and feeling unable to effect any change in our lives.

However, in my opinion, it can never be truly healing to such a person to help them regain a sense of personal power and control over themselves and their lives through dominating and controlling another being; in our case, the horse. It is beyond short-sighted to use techniques which promote the control of another sentient being and to advocate the use of force and domination in an attempt at healing. Surely the only benefits here are a very short-lived boost of adrenaline and a sense of having gained some degree of control again, along with a momentary boost of confidence and sense of security. It can never be ethical or truly healing, in my view, to benefit one species through the subjugation of another.

Instead, we should be aiming to assist the client to really access their lost power and potency. However, to do that requires the courage and support to go inside and *be with* our powerlessness in the presence of the horse and facilitator. It is absolutely not okay to force *another* being into a place of powerlessness in order to regain our *own* power. In fact, this either compounds, rather than heals the wounds in people obtained through excessively dominant, violent and controlled experiences or simply encourages the perpetuation of the same modus operandi they are used to employing in their lives. Change can only be minimal at best in such circumstances.

What I have seen being employed in some areas of equine facilitated practice are pretty forceful approaches to moving a horse loose around a round pen or arena. Clients are being shown the rudimentary basics of how to do so. Then they are sent in before they are fully able to modulate their own arousal and energy levels, stay connected to their body and their emotions, be assertive with true confidence rather than force, and ask by using energy and breath; rather than chasing a horse with a rope or whip. Lacking the subtle awareness of these elements as discussed throughout this book, clients are being taught nothing but the mechanics of how to do this and through a continuation of the old school dominance-submission tactics. They are not focusing on relationship; either self-relationship or relationship to another sentient being. Nor are they learning how to lead softly without pressure and force, which involves asking and two-way communication, rather than telling. Unfortunately, when skimming the surface this way, practitioners are in danger of embedding old habits in people. While in addition, promoting the seemingly quick-fix benefits of increased confidence and connection when the horse moves away 'successfully', or comes towards them and 'joins-up' through submission and fear, rather than free will and choice.

So, it is very clear to me that if we involve active round pen sessions with horses in our equine facilitated work, then we need to be doing this carefully and only as part of a wide range of practice, (for example, see also the earlier section on employing more reflective rather than active sessions). Above all, we need to be doing this in a gentle and respectful way to the horses we work with. Otherwise we end up with potentially stale, resentful horses who do become subjected to clients' mixed emotions, mixed intentions and potentially dominant tactics even if unintentionally. So it is beholden on us as the facilitator to model and carefully show clients how to do things a different way.

In the award winning short film, *White Mane*, by French filmmaker, Albert Lamorisse, there is a vivid depiction of the two contrasting approaches I have been describing – the old fashioned dominance-submission approach to handling horses, or the gentler, kinder approach that I am encouraging. In this beautiful film, which is set in the Camargue region of France, a group of local men try to catch and tame a wild Camargue stallion, called White Mane. When they finally succeed in herding him into a large round pen, the horse manages to escape their dominance and forceful use of ropes and whips, jumping out of the pen. Some time later, a young boy gently and sensitively manages to connect with and even ride White Mane. Using a completely different approach, without any force, the boy does what I am suggesting *is* possible with horses. By relating to them in truly horse-like ways without force or aggression, but rather through heart-based intention, love, respect and sensitivity then, in my experience, horses often choose to join us, as this stallion did with his young rider.

I have had a number of similar, if less dramatic, experiences myself with semi-wild horses. Through employing this softer, more respectful approach, they often come very close to me, walk beside me, enjoy a mutual groom or are just happy for us to share the same environment. I can only imagine that running after them waving a rope and putting them under pressure, would indeed make them head for the hills, and I would have blown my chance completely to be close to them.

However, as I suggested earlier, all of this requires much more focus on yourself and your own inner process and much less on controlling, changing or training the horse. It is inevitably the more difficult path for us to take initially, but the results for you and most especially the horses, are limitless as this approach garners trust in you by a significantly larger, more powerful animal, with finely tuned instincts and flight or fight responses intact. To create such a relationship, where anything is possible with your horse... now that *is* exciting, stress-free and joyful.

Chapter 15

General Care and Consideration of the Horses in Equine Facilitated Practice

Throughout this book I have outlined what I feel are many of the necessary elements to deliver good quality equine facilitated practice. This approach is respectful of the horses, provides the conditions for empowered horses to help people to their maximum ability, and is in no sense detrimental to the well-being of the horses.

To review, some of the key elements of this approach are:

1. Honoring our horses as full partners in our work together rather than employing them as 'tools', simply to obtain outcomes for clients or practitioners regardless of the impact on them.

2. Respecting horses as sentient beings in their own right with a destiny of their own and allowing them as much choice as possible.

3. Undertaking our ongoing personal development so that we are consciously honing our body-awareness and developing emotional agility skills. Ensuring we are therefore more body-centered and congruent in our interactions with our horses which permeates our entire facilitating approach.

4. Developing energetic awareness and sensitivity so that we can relate to horses in a way that they understand and respond well to. This also ensures that we can support our horses fully in sessions through our subtle attunement to their energy and that of our colleagues and clients. This ultimately enables us to also best support our clients.

5. Working consistently at respecting the horses' physical, emotional and spiritual boundaries and not interfering in the process between horses and clients through our

own projections, interjections, agenda, and outcome or ego-driven needs.

When we are incorporating these core elements, then I believe we are creating a true, inter-species partnership that inevitably means healthy and happy horses who are capable of supporting people. Through partnering with horses in this way we can minimize our own and our clients' impact on them and not leave them with additional 'baggage' which creates stress or ill-health in them.

In this final chapter I take a look at some of the more general aspects of caring for our equine partners; choosing which horses to work with and the types of suitable environments for carrying out equine facilitated work. My suggestions here are what I believe creates the optimum conditions to best support our equine partners. Further, given the type of work we are asking our horses to carry out, it feels even more important to me that we enable them to live as natural and peaceful a lifestyle as possible. However, I also recognize that there are many different approaches to horse care and for some people, choosing different management lifestyle approaches will work best for them and their horses.

Care and Support of the Horses

In terms of day-to-day care of the horses, there is an enormous amount of information available to horse owners nowadays about all aspects of horse care. So while this is available, should you choose to avail yourself of it, I personally feel that keeping horses healthy and happy is actually very simple and can be the most cost-effective way of owning horses, too. Simple really is best when it comes to horses. We have over-complicated the care of our horses, driven by the enormous market for supplements, feeds, equipment and training gadgets, much of which is just that, a market driven by profit rather than what is actually best for the horses. When living in the wild, horses live very simply and so it is far better to not overly confuse their digestive, immune and musculoskeletal systems, causing negative impacts on their psychological and emotional well-being, as well as difficult behaviors. I therefore feel that the more naturally and simply we can keep our horses, the better.

In addition to the five core elements listed above, I have found that there are five further management approaches that specifically enable our equine facilitated partners to have as natural and happy a lifestyle as possible within a domesticated setting.

First, our horses need to live as part of a herd. Horses in isolation without herd members suffer in many ways and it is advisable to never keep your horse on his own. Horses need, at the very least, one other herd mate to feel safe and happy through having company and communication with another horse. In particular, when undertaking this work, maintaining a settled herd with minimal changes and minimal time separating any individual horse, is vital to their well-being. I find that this single factor can have immense repercussions on horses' health, perhaps more so than we have previously understood or wanted to accept.

I found with my horses that it was very important to them to always be kept together as a herd, whether when turned out, or when they came in to work with clients, or to be exercised. Any substantial degree of separation seemed to affect all of them and disrupt their normal state of equilibrium. They ranged in varying degrees from LP, who was somewhat agreeable to going out for a ride on her own, through to North who would become beside himself with anxiety if he was taken away from his herd. A normally quiet, easy going horse, he would become very distraught due to separation anxiety. To this end, then, I made sure that the herd was not adversely disrupted for the majority of the time, and spent time gradually acclimatizing my horses to working one-to-one, either with just me or with our clients *within the vicinity* of the rest of the herd. This gave them the security that they clearly needed; to know that they would be coming back to their herd members at the end of the session. I was fortunate in that I had use of a yard with an arena, paddock and stabling all close by, which made this possible. I found with my horses that when they expressed their distress at being separated *and* I listened, that this was a key factor to maintaining their overall wellness and keeping their levels of stress to a minimum. Obviously, a large part of what we were together to do, was to provide a calm, safe space for clients. Keeping the herd balanced and happy was therefore of paramount importance.

In recent years I have also spent some time observing feral herds of ponies in the New Forest. It was clear to me that them being in their relatively constant herds was the main contributing factor to their sense of safety and palpable state of equilibrium. I spent hours on end watching them and found that these ponies were always either in their herd or grazing nearby; never did I come across a solitary pony. All of which has led me to reflect more deeply on our very human tendency to move our horses from herd to herd. This is often more about meeting our needs, rather than really meeting those of our horses and doing what is best for them. There are times when, unfortunately, we face little choice but to separate horses and move our horse to another facility or perhaps out of their herd. Often for financial reasons or significant life-changing circumstances, we are sometimes forced to wrench them apart. But when this isn't the case, then enabling a herd to live undisturbed makes a significant difference to each horse's emotional and physical well-being. Horses have a complex social life with each other that they work out in ways we are only just now beginning to understand. When we interfere with this according to our needs and goals, we can cause untold stress and ill-health in horses, often without realizing just how much.

Second, from my experience and understanding it is far more preferable that horses live out all year round, as far as possible, with access to a continual supply of food (roughage in the forms of grass or hay), water and shelter.

Movement and continual access to food for grazing herd animals is of paramount importance to maintain well-being on all levels. Horses' digestive, immune, respiratory and musculoskeletal systems all evolved to support their nomadic way of life: to move and to eat. Domesticating horses and keeping them in confined spaces and with restricted feeding are the very worst things we can do and then expect our horse's health to be good. To expect an animal that has evolved, survived and thrived for millions of years to adapt to meet our human agendas and environments is clearly highly counter-productive if we want the healthiest equine partners possible. Thankfully, now, there is a large movement towards keeping domestic horses in more natural ways, and especially towards adhering to these two fundamental areas of horse needs: To live as herds and to live out with continual access to food and water. By keeping horses in stables in order to make it more convenient for us, or to meet a projected human need in us that we place onto them, we actually *create* enormous problems in terms of our horse's mental, emotional and physical health. We also risk creating complex unnecessary behaviors that we then need to spend a fortune on trying to 'fix' in our horses, through equipment or training. Humans can be our own and other species' worst enemies, as we have a tendency to create overly complex situations that can easily be avoided if we just keep things simple.

On a practical note, if the amount of land you have is limited and for most horse owners this is the case, then I highly recommend implementing the *Paddock Paradise System* developed by Jaime Jackson. Jaime's book, *Paddock Paradise: A Guide to Natural Horse Boarding* is a great resource to have. This is an excellent way of allowing your horses to have maximum movement and grazing through a 'track system' that you create in your fields. I have seen a number of herds living like this and it seems to make for very healthy and relaxed horses, as well as making a few acres go a long way. Jackson's approach turns much of traditional horse care upside down and brings it as close to natural conditions as possible within domesticated settings. His advice helps horse owners care much more holistically for their horses' diet, fitness and in particular, their hooves, in simple yet effective ways. Jackson's track system arose following his own observations and research into how feral herds lived. Specifically, he noticed how these horses didn't seem to suffer from chronic lameness issues that many domesticated horses do, such as navicular or laminitis. He began experimenting with removing shoes from horses and trimming their hooves to reflect the natural hoof. He then developed the track system to stimulate movement and on different surfaces, much as feral or wild horses' hooves encounter all day, every day.

Here's what one person says about using a track system:

'I have my horses barefoot, and maximizing movement to get them as healthy as possible was key. I love the idea of the Paddock Paradise System, and although we didn't get it to work completely as described in the book due to the make-up of our land, I still think it's an excellent way to make use of the pastures. Make sure you put something attractive at the far end of your system so that the horses will work a little to get to (for example the hay station or hay nets), especially if you have 'obstacles' such as difficult terrain between the shed and the far end. If you can, it's a good idea to put fine gravel on wet spots and around any area that gets laden with manure. For us it turns out that the spacing apart of 'attractors' such as feed, water and so on, did more to optimize movement than did having a track. We already had them on 24/7 turnout. However, I still think it's a great way to use the land and would definitely recommend anyone to try it, but to tweak the Paddock Paradise System to your needs and your own conditions.'

A third essential management approach, in my view, in caring for our equine facilitated partners, is that the horses we work with are turned out into their field and herd immediately at the end of each session. This is a vital element in this work for our horses' continued well-being, enjoyment and ability to 'go back to grazing'. Horses live moment by moment, so if they need to shake something off, they need to do so immediately. For them to hold onto their impulse to move, roll or graze is not in their best interest and is a sure-fire way to them becoming stale and potentially negatively impacted in some way. Further, as we are often requiring them to enter our artificial environments, such as outdoor or indoor riding arenas, to do this type of work, then taking them back into their own environment as soon as the session is over is really important.

The end of session also preferably means the end of the horses' actual interaction with the client, rather than the formal end of the session. I understand this may not always be possible, especially if we are working alone. It is very important that we do not allow the horses' well-being to slip down our list of priorities as we carry out our work, or stand around chatting at the end of the session. It is easy to do so, especially if we are very busy, but ensuring that we are being mindful in each moment of our horses' needs is essential, ethical and respectful, in order to maintain healthy and happy equine partners. My experience is that horses are often happy to step forward and carry out this work, but they equally need and want to return to their herd as soon as their job is done.

One final thought here is, that I have also found that when it is necessary to attend to the horse's needs during a session, this can be an important part of the process for our clients too. We are then modeling doing things properly in terms of taking good care of our work colleagues. This demonstrates attentiveness, empathy, consideration and self-care for our clients.

Fourth, that the horses we work with have a varied lifestyle. This should include substantial time just being a horse in their herd, with minimal human contact, but also time spent with us in relaxing modes such as meditation, play and exercise, all of which ensures that they have a good balance of work, rest and play.

Common sense needs to prevail in terms of sensibly scheduling sessions per day, week, month and year. Find the balance that seems to work for you and your horses. Ensure they have non-work activities, too, whether riding, round pen work with you, driving, whatever else it is you like doing together, and always ensure they have complete periods off. Rotate the horses used in your practice if you have a large enough herd. If you have a small herd, work in such a way that the horses have maximum choice about whether they work or not on that day. You can do this by letting them be loose in their field, or an arena and let the horse choose the client, if appropriate. One of the key concerns being presently reported and which is ripe for further research, is assessing how frequently good therapy horses are being repeatedly used in this work. There is a high risk of such horses being over-used and therefore the risk of burn-out or ill-heath in these horses is also probably higher.[11]

In terms of workload with my own herd, we found a happy balance of work, rest and play. I learned to pay close attention to my own energy levels and I quickly found out what my own capacity was to work with clients each day and week. Parallel to this, I was also paying close attention to how often the horses were working with people. I scheduled sessions so that they were evenly paced, with plenty of space in between and regularly included complete weekends and weeks off. I would also just play with my horses, both in the field and in the lovely big outdoor arena we had use of. I would relax, hang out with them or do some loose active work, or put music on and move around with one of them. In the field, I would spend time just sitting quietly or giving one of them a good scratch when requested.

Fifth, the horse's health is maintained through natural methods as far as possible, in conjunction with mainstream veterinary care of course, when necessary.

The following are some of the complementary methods I have found helpful to maintaining horses' well-being: Herbs; essential oils; homeopathy; chiropractic or physiotherapy treatments; massage; Reiki; energy rebalancing; kinesiology; shamanic healing and drumming. Obviously, it is imperative to employ fully trained and recommended therapists in these methods. A word-of-mouth recommendation is the most trustworthy, I find. Horses respond extremely well to natural remedies, such as herbs and essential oils. This is because these are the ways in which they would care for themselves in the wild. For example, they self-select the natural herbage and minerals that they need from the varied foliage, as they graze and move. In a single field, horses cannot access the same variety and so we need to offer them supplements or take them out regularly and allow them to forage on a walk or gentle hack. A friend of mine often takes her gelding out for a gentle amble and lets him self-select what he wants from the hedges, trees and grasses. How refreshing, compared to the more traditional equestrian's approach when out hacking to 'never let the horse eat!' Horses are often punished if they try to do so, yet they are simply doing what comes completely naturally to them. If we restrict their dietary intake then we must allow them to obtain what they need on a regular basis, just as they would in the wild.

One of my favorite complementary remedies to offer to horses is essential oils. Offering a range of different oils at different times allows the horse to choose what she intuitively knows she needs on that occasion. When the horse really needs a particular property in an oil, she will inhale it or even ingest it by licking it from your hand. Occasionally, they may indicate they need the oil applying topically to a part of their body, too. Essential oils work on all levels and facilitate releases in horses emotionally, physically and spiritually, making them a great balancing remedy to use regularly. Plus they smell wonderful and I often found that whatever my horses chose, I often needed a good dose of as well, so we both benefited. Obviously, it is important to employ a fully trained practitioner in safely administering essential oils, as they need to be carefully blended and diluted. Or you could undertake some training yourself to learn how to administer them and understand the horse's responses. Please do not simply buy some and offer them to your horse yourself, as they can be toxic and cause burns if incorrectly diluted.

Being highly sensitive animals, horses also respond exceptionally well to any type of energy healing such as Reiki and massage, hands-on healing or indeed any form of 'subtle medicine' such as shamanic healing. Any of these are wonderful ways to further support out equine colleagues.

Recently, I have become aware through a friend and colleague's work that horses can benefit from shamanic drumming. Graeme Green of *The Mindful Horse* provides a range of distance healing for horses, including shamanic healing and chakra balancing. He has also recently been exploring the health benefits to horses of using a shaman's drum to help restore the horse's well-being. Having undertaken some drumming with horses on my own and with Graeme, it seems as though the vibrational energy released from the rhythmical drumming facilitates an energetic, emotional and physical release in the horse. I have seen horses licking and chewing, yawning, entering a very relaxed, almost trance-like state and even lying down to sleep or roll during a period of drumming. In Graeme's words: '*In our drumming we create a space for the horse. A place which the horse may or may not choose to enter, it is their decision as to how to interact. They know their needs. This is a place without demand or agenda, nothing beyond the benefit of the intention we create beneath the drumming. Sometimes that gift is healing in itself.*' One horse I drummed with began by rubbing his face and head all along the drum, then one side of his entire body, until he then backed up into the drum in my hand and practically sat on it as I tried to continue drumming. The horse took a few rapid breaths and then let out a deep sigh and walked away. In just a few minutes he had asked for and released something he was ready to let go of and then, of course, simply went back to grazing.

I have found that by employing these five management approaches, in addition to the way we partner with our horses as advocated throughout, then our horses tend to be happy, healthy and willing to help us support our clients.

Which Horses to Partner With?

When forming a herd, it is useful to have a good mix of horses, including different temperaments, types, sizes and ages. This creates a wider spectrum to work with different clients and client types. It also opens up more possibilities for the clients to explore in terms of who they are attracted to or not, and why, and the range of potential issues or resonance is greater. All horses have unique personalities, backgrounds and preferences, just as we do.

In my experience, there is no *type* of horse that is either good or bad for equine facilitated practice. No particular breed or type is better than another, or suitable for particular client groups. There are some exceptions here, of course, for example, small ponies can often be very helpful when working with children or very nervous clients. I have worked across a vast range of horse breeds and found that healing is often very possible, no matter the type of horse. At the beautiful mountain ranch in Arizona where Eponaquest® used to be based and where I trained, the herd included a rich variety of horses such as Quarter horses, Percherons, Thoroughbreds, Egyptian Arabians, Dutch Warmbloods and Appaloosas, to name a few.

From miniature Shetlands, donkeys and native horses and ponies, to cobs of all types and draft horses, horses are horses and bring their innate healing potential, regardless of their breeding, original purpose or training. However, there are real considerations about particular individual horses, their behavior and background, which need to be considered fully before embarking on sensitive healing work between horses and people.

As I talked about in Chapter 4, where I explored the idea of horses as sentient beings, it is my experience that, a lot of the time, horses find us to do this type of work together. They make their way into our lives somehow, usually through a series of synchronicities. But I also recognize that this isn't always the way it happens, or isn't how some people would see this. Therefore, if you prefer to take the more practical route and look for horses in a more conventional way, or start working with the horses you already own or have access to, then here are some key considerations when looking for equine partners for your practice. Of course, these all apply too even if your horses 'find' you.

First, what is your personal response to this horse? Do you like him or not? Do you easily connect with him? What do you sense or intuit about him? How does he make you feel? What emotions come up? What memories? Pay attention to how your body feels around him. If you are tense, stiff and not relaxed around him, then use that as information. Let your body, emotions and senses all guide you and try not to make the decision solely based on economic factors or practical issues like size, or age of horse. Instead, trust your gut about that particular horse and your response to him.

Second, it is obviously very important in this work to check that the horse does not presently exhibit dangerous behaviors towards people, for example, biting, kicking, rearing, charging, running off or barging into people.

Third, the horse is interested in and generally likes people. Some horses are much more interested in connecting with people than others. However, most horses usually are interested to varying degrees when they have been treated respectfully by people. But if they are not, for whatever reason, they may not be suitable for sustained and regular interactions with people, and especially groups of people. They may have unresolved trauma or pain themselves that needs attending to first, or they may simply not be wishing to engage closely with people, due to their history or personal preferences. Therefore, it is important to recognize and respect that not all horses want to do this work.

Fourth, that the horses we work with must not have been conditioned to expect food treats. This is obviously vital in this work as we are introducing new people in the form of our clients all the time to our horses. The last thing that should be happening is that the horses harass the clients for food treats. Nibbling in pockets and pushing people's boundaries in expectation or even demand of food, is highly undesirable. To this end, I do not involve food in any capacity in this work.

I would like to make a more general observation here too on the issue of food in this work with horses. Contrary to some equestrian training and some equine facilitated approaches, I feel it is highly dangerous territory to introduce the concept of food as an inducement or reward for their work. Food plays a complex and important role in the lives of horses as it is central to their survival and well-being. In the wild, horses need to ensure they have access to food at all times. When in domesticated settings, this freedom to find their own food is severely restricted, and they are often wholly dependent on us to stay alive. Yet there is a long-standing habit in equestrianism to use food as an incentive and/or reward in horse training. I am completely opposed to this as I feel it interferes with one of the horse's key primal needs to survive as well as their entire metabolic system. It also adds a further unnecessary layer of control over our horses if we use food to punish or reward. Further, I believe it develops 'learned helplessness' in our horses. It can also very quickly create pushy and dangerous horses in my experience. This is obviously a complex issue which I don't have scope to explore in more detail here. Suffice to say, my advice is to avoid treats or food-based games of any kind in equine facilitated work and ensure that the horses you work with are not likely to aggressively demand treats from unsuspecting clients.

Fifth, finding out about the background of the horse as far as possible is also helpful, especially checking whether there is a history of abuse by people and if so, what form of abuse. This is so that you know the likely triggers for that horse. For example, the use of a stick, rope or even wearing a particular hat, could trigger a memory of former abuse in a horse. Consider employing an intuitive animal communicator or shamanic practitioner if you are not confident of doing this yourself, to get a glimpse into the horse's background, especially if no history is passed on with the horse. This is often the case in rescued horses, or those who have been sold many times. It is also always important to ask about early experiences of that horse, such as when and how were they weaned, and how they were originally handled and backed by humans. As with people, many horses' issues can be connected back to their early life experiences, especially with their mother *and* with their primary human handlers and trainers.

It is important not to interpret very quiet horses to be just that. They could well be shut down, traumatized or dissociated through past experiences. Riding school horses, racehorses, or some competition horses are often in this state following years of pressurized lifestyles and handling. If you have the time and desire to rehabilitate such a horse who you also get a good feeling about, then they may indeed make a very good therapy horse, as in the case of my experience with North Star.

Horses who don't seem able to offer their abilities freely, may be too shut down or traumatized to do this work at all, and in need of their own healing and rehabilitation first. I do not believe it is fair to ask them to give when they need healing themselves, unless they show clear signs of wanting to do this work. Their healing must happen first if it seems the horse could be suitable. Further, they will not be able to give you overt and clear feedback about their own needs while in such a state, and therefore it can be hard to determine what they are also mirroring in the client. Horses in this state, if allowed to rest and recover while also being offered healing can, in time, indicate a desire to work with people. Left out in their herd as they are rehabilitated, they can then choose to come over to the fence-line or not when a client arrives, without putting them under any pressure. I have known such horses to gradually indicate an interest in the work once they begin to feel better in themselves and when given choice and freedom to come and go around people we are working with.

New initiatives are springing up around the world where horses that need rehabilitation are being paired with humans in recovery, with the aim being mutual healing. However, I am personally very cautious about these pairings as a single approach or program.

My bottom line is that the horses we ask to support vulnerable people, some of whom have severe emotional and psychological problems, should be well and healed themselves first. No doubt there is some degree of mutual healing going on in some cases. However, I have a lot of reservations about this approach. My experience of working with rescued horses in need of rehabilitation is that any engagement with troubled people needs to be done carefully and gently, and also must not be the main type of clients that they engage with regularly. In addition, traditional and some natural horsemanship approaches will not work well in this case, as the horses will be either highly resistant to further dominance-based tactics, or potentially further harmed. They certainly won't be easily able to step into their full power once more. Undoubtedly there will be considerable emotional resonance going on between these horses and clients, making this seem like a good pairing on the surface, but again I ask, what about the impact on the horses?

A further thought on resonance here. In my experience, it is undeniably the case that some horses that have been abused or suffered trauma *can* make excellent equine facilitated partners; but not all. So while great caution is advised don't write them off, either, because of this. I have trained and worked with horses who have recovered from severe traumas or illnesses, as well as horses with sight in only one eye, former racehorses, and those who have been very badly backed as youngsters or physically abused by people. Even when overt trauma or abuse is not obvious or known in a horse's history, poor and overly aggressive or rough handling can lead these sensitive and normally gentle animals, to suffer intense misery and fear. Unfortunately, this is still hugely prevalent in the horse world, However, I have witnessed and experienced many such horses choose a particular client who has a similar history or present state to work with and seen nothing short of deep and profound healing take place between these two injured beings. When a traumatized person is actively chosen by a horse of that horse's free will, and given the healing support and space they both need, significant mutual healing often takes place. In the horse offering support to the person, they seem to catch a ride on the healing taking place, often releasing emotional and physical traumas at the same time. However, as I have reiterated throughout, *how* this takes place and the approach used is key to ensuring the horses do not inadvertently endure further suffering, albeit through well-intentioned desires to help people in need. Similarly, the amount of time engaged with such clients must be kept to a minimum to avoid burn-out in the horses, which is another reason why the new initiatives mentioned previously cause me concern. Ideally a mix of clients is preferable which allows for including some lighter, more fun-based sessions to avoid the heaviness of some sessions, and potential risk of staleness in the horses.

Sixth, how is the horse when you do simple handling tasks when you visit her? When you approach her, how does she respond? Is she curious about a new human? Or impassive, scared or aggressive? When in close proximity, does she push into your space repeatedly, even when you set a boundary? When you lead her, does she pull you, or walk into you? How is she to groom? How is she when loose in an arena or round pen? As far as possible, undertake some simple horsemanship tasks with her. Also notice how she is when loose in both her field and in an arena. Try some active round pen work with her, too, to see how she may have been previously trained and what her level of interest or sourness is in this regard.

The seventh factor is the age of the horse: For this type of work I do not feel it is advisable to have young, unhandled horses in your herd, especially if you also work with your clients with the horses in a herd environment in their field. This is obviously a safety issue for your clients, as young horses can be unpredictable and overly curious. They also have a tendency to nip, 'mouth' (chewing on items), and can continually push into people's space, as they themselves are still learning about appropriate boundaries. Again, as with much of this work, for some clients this may well be the medicine they need. However, for more nervous or vulnerable clients this is not desirable. In addition to the consideration of your clients, though, is the impact on the young horse. Asking them to do this work before they are ready and able to, is far from ideal. It may be possible to gradually allow them to be part of the herd for observational activities. However, I suggest not using them for one-to-one or group sessions other than through observation, or when doing Meet the Herd *over* a fence-line, until they are able to respond to boundary setting and you know they are safe around people.

As with everything in this work, it is the facilitator's responsibility to keep their clients safe at all times. Of course things can suddenly just happen when around horses, but by carrying out thorough risk-assessments beforehand, you can minimize the obvious risks, and young horses invariably bring additional risks.

Further, young horses are developing physically, emotionally and psychologically, so the amount of 'work' they do, especially if also in the process of being backed for riding, needs to be carefully managed. Don't overwhelm young horses by exposing them to deep work with clients too soon. The last thing you want to do is confuse that horse or turn him sour through giving his brain and nervous system too much to process too quickly. Little and often while also allowing as much choice as possible, are the key considerations with youngsters.

One last but major consideration for effectively partnering with horses in equine facilitated practice is *where* you and your horses work, so I shall now explore suitable facilities and environments for sessions.

Suitable Facilities for Equine Facilitated Practice

One of the key physical and practical elements of offering equine facilitated practice is having a suitable venue.

Having worked both freelance and on my own yard delivering EFL, I can say that it is by far preferable to have sole control of a facility if you are offering equine facilitated services. There are pros and cons, as having your own facility is costly and a significant overhead to regularly cover, but the benefits of being able to create a conducive environment and deliver your service uninhibited by other yard users and activities, are substantial. To effectively deliver this sensitive work requires privacy, peace and quiet and importantly, the ability to maintain confidentiality.

Many clients seek out this form of help as they are looking for an alternative to more traditional talk-based therapies. Horses offer a medium of safety through their non-judgmental attitudes and so this reassures people who have experienced mistrust of other people. To reveal deep-seated scars and traumas in front of others can be challenging for many, so to be able to provide a private, quiet space where interruptions are minimized is essential.

I have also worked on a variety of facilities, including riding schools, livery yards, privately owned stables, competition yards, therapeutic riding centers and other equine facilitated centers. However, it has often been a struggle to ensure the type of set-up where you can allow both the horses' maximum choice and the type of privacy and non-interrupted time that you and your clients need. I have found that one of the most important elements in making this happen is that the owner of the facility fully understands the nature of this work. It is preferable that they have been a client of this method themselves and so they know first-hand how vulnerable people can feel. Without this degree of understanding, there is the potential for unintended disruptions, changes to herds, additions to personalities on a yard, equine and human, as well as potentially over-booking a facility's schedule.

Some practitioners are finding that a solution to these two options is to share facilities. The benefits to this option I feel are significant, as of course the appreciable overheads involved in keeping horses and a facility can be shared and so kept down. But it also streamlines the number of facilities offering similar services as opposed to hundreds of small organizations springing up. I personally feel this is a very sensible approach to more efficient delivery of this work, particularly in terms of making services financially viable. The biggest additional consideration this inevitably brings, however, is the workload of the horses if the herd is being shared. Or, if a second herd is brought in, then it becomes an issue of adequate grazing land which needs to be able to sustain your horses living out all year round, as far as possible. It is a delicate balance to accommodate all of these requirements, but the support and partnership that comes from working alongside other practitioners can be invaluable. The financial requirements and pressures of running any service where horses are a core element are never to be underestimated.

In terms of what is needed in a facility though, you really don't need expensive top of the range facilities to do this work effectively.

The essential equine requirements are: Access to horses who have indicated a desire to do this work and preferably who have freedom of movement to employ this choice, plus a round pen, or an arena, or a fenced-off enclosure in a field to do one-to-one sessions. I have found that an indoor arena is not essential. I have worked all year round with just an outdoor arena and in fact, nowadays I prefer not to use indoor arenas as I find they can hold stale energy and take the horses into too much of an unnatural environment, particularly for this type of deep, emotional work.

When you are setting up your work spaces, consider how long the horses will be involved and have a plan for ensuring they are attended to throughout the session. This is especially important for longer sessions like full day workshops or practitioner training programs. Therefore, employing a dedicated horse handler is essential for group sessions, workshops and training courses and is invaluable for the health and welfare of your horses.

I feel that it is preferable when you take one horse out of their herd to do a one-to-one with a client, the horse can still see his herd, (another reason why I don't like indoor arenas as they immediately remove this option for the horse). This is the ideal set-up to ensure the horse feels relaxed enough to focus on the client. If the horse's own arousal level is high due to his separation anxiety, then he will not be able to engage with your client fully. Take this into consideration when you are setting up your work space. Also take into account access to food and water during the times the horse/s is working. Keep water available at all times and feed beforehand so the horse isn't getting hungry as the hours tick away; remembering they are grazers and so require access to forage all the time except for brief periods.

I have carried out some of my work in fields and in some ways, I prefer to do this now. I find being out in nature and in the horse's environment puts us on much more of a level playing ground with the horses. It also tends to lead to a much more relaxed and natural experience for my clients and myself. Here, we can work with the horses more on *their* terms rather than on ours. It is becoming more widely acknowledged nowadays that simply being outside in a natural environment is greatly healing for people, especially for those with mental and emotional health needs. Further, in the context of this work, what is so advantageous about this, is that as the horses are in *their* environment they therefore have more freedom of movement and choice as the whole herd can take part in choosing who works with which client. The more I have experimented with working in different settings and most particularly since working in the expanse of the New Forest National Park with the free roaming herds of ponies, the more I find myself preferring to be out in fields with the horses.

The biggest consideration in doing this, of course, is the safety of your clients. Therefore, moving into working with clients in a field with a herd of loose horses is to be approached carefully and thoroughly, with safety being paramount throughout; remembering that this will definitely not be suitable for all clients. As I have described in Chapter 4, with an exercise such as Meet the Herd, this can best be done over a fence with a herd, so that participants are not in danger and they can focus more fully on themselves. Additionally, my preference when working with clients is to take them through the steps involved in learning how to set healthy boundaries with horses, as well as sensing the horses' boundaries.

Then, once this is established, it is much safer to take *some* clients into a field with a herd. It is all a matter of common sense. An alternative and effective approach is to create a fenced area in your field to work with a single horse. This deals with the issue of the safety of your client around an entire herd, but also enables that horse to be in close proximity to her herd and therefore feel more content to focus on her work.

In addition to the space for the equine work itself, you will also need the following: A warm, dry indoor space to sit and talk with clients – anything from a dry barn or tack room to a yurt, tipi, kitchen or classroom can work for this; toilet facilities, and a kitchen for group workshops, so that you can provide water and hot drinks at the very least. Refreshments are important, especially for day-long workshops as people are doing deep psychological and emotional work and so require energy-providing snacks and warm drinks to keep hydrated, replenished and grounded. Clients cannot concentrate or let themselves drop into a place of vulnerability if they are cold, thirsty or needing to use the bathroom. Remembering Maslow's hierarchy of need helps here; if our basic human needs are not being met, we cannot move into the deeper realms of self-discovery, as our focus is on our physical needs and their associated emotional and psychological needs and complexes.

Finally, there is one other issue I would like to consider concerning suitable environments for undertaking this work. In recent years there has been an increase in the practice of taking horses into human environments to offer therapeutic support to those who are unable to go out, for example, taking horses into residential and nursing homes. Now, while I have no doubt that some gentle, genuine healing takes place for those people unable to leave such environments, as this may be the only contact they now have with the natural world, I am concerned again about the impact on the horses involved. In these situations, we are taking them completely out of their 'natural' environment into an entirely human one. Further still, there are some who now even take horses to places such as business parks, hotels and universities to carry out EFL, leadership and team-building sessions.

My first concern around this particular development is that we are taking these sensitive, non-predatory mammals into unnatural, built-up, possibly noisy environments, with sometimes intense levels of energy. This is potentially frightening and stressful to them, especially to horses who have little or no tendency to shut down. Which takes us back to the debate around whether we want to strive for compliant or empowered equine partners in our work. My second concern is that, one of the key factors that has made equine facilitated support so beneficial to many different groups of people, is that it allows people to leave their usual built-up environments and enter the horses' world. It is now commonly acknowledged that simply being outdoors and in nature is greatly therapeutic in itself. Why then remove this valuable element for the people and ask the horses to instead meet us more than halfway again? My experience has shown me that when we strive to enter the horse's world more fully then we are really able to reach a much more balanced place in ourselves. My final concern with this approach is that, it feels, again to me, like a continuation of the top-down approach, where we make the choices and our horses comply to fit in with our desires and we are not therefore shifting ourselves as the horses are suggesting.

If we wish to introduce the healing power of nature and animals to those who may not be fit or able to leave their indoor environment, then I would ask, is a horse the most appropriate animal for this person to be in connection with? Would it perhaps be just as positive an experience for that person to engage with an animal which is far more comfortable in indoor human environments such as a dog or cat?

In terms of this development, then, is it truly fair that we then expect these horses to support people, when their basic needs and stress levels have been potentially affected? Research into the impact on the horses undertaking this type of equine facilitated work would be very helpful to determine how the horses carrying out this type of work are coping with this. My gut feeling says this is not the way forward and instead, we must continue to hold true to the suggestions from the horses. That we need to step out of our concrete environments as far as possible and remember that we, too, belong and indeed thrive, in nature. As the human element of this inter-species partnership, this is one of the times when we can definitely lead the way by remembering the purpose of this work in its wider context. We can do this by encouraging people back into nature, to find the healing and balance that is missing for so many in today's modern world, and strive to enter the horse's world as much as possible. I feel it is time to meet the horses more on their ground if we are ever going to truly shift and heal as a species.

CONCLUSIONS

When the considerations I have explored throughout are well met, then I believe we are in a good position to offer equine facilitated services to people while being confident we have happy, empowered horses as our partners. When our horses are well cared for and involved throughout in a respectful and honored way, where they are allowed to step into their power and able to express themselves fully rather than being submissive, compliant or having to shut down their impulses and emotions; then we can feel confident that we are doing our best by them and our clients.

Overall, what is most required by the human facilitator partnering with horses is that they surrender their ego to the process. When we do this, our purer soul-essence, which doesn't seek control, is then able to step forward and partner with these magnificent, generous animals in harmony. The horses are much more attracted to this part of us and so happily join us in our work to support people through their learning and healing. This is the essence of a true human-equine working partnership, then; where marvelous deep healing can occur and where we truly join with horses and 'the magic' happens.

To do anything less than this makes a nonsense of involving horses. To not move ourselves and our willing, brave clients into a more horse-like way of living, through developing emotional intelligence, embodied living and non-dominant approaches to relationships, is to reject the very lessons horses seem willing to teach us.

We have to constantly remind ourselves that this method came from the horses themselves. This truly is Horse Medicine that we are trading in. As the practitioner, we are the vessel for the slow releasing of this medicine for those who come to us to partake of it.

What all of this comes down to, ultimately, is to approach our horses with unconditional love and gratitude for their support and guidance. When we fill our hearts with love and gratitude, I can guarantee that the horses will respond positively to us. We must be ever vigilant not to turn them into the tools of our trade once again, but uphold a reverence and respect for them and continually convey this through loving kindness and a gentle, wholly respectful working approach.

In the end, our horses will show us the way, as they have been patiently trying to do for so long in our enduring relationship with them, which has lasted for centuries. What is beholden on us is to listen and be willing to let them take the reins at times in our partnership through the wonderful, rewarding and deeply moving work that is equine facilitated growth. Without the horses and their innate abilities to help people, we can only offer a fraction of what seems so essential for many people. Humanity needs more than ever to foster a big heart, a deeper connection to our bodies, our emotions, one another and our natural world if we are going to survive and live fulfilling lives. What we are going to need is to be like the horse; a gentle, peaceful animal that lives in harmony with others and embodies qualities long since forgotten in the human psyche. We need the horses now more than ever.

Afterword

In the uncanny way that things tend to unfold in my life now, just as I was entering the final stages of editing this book I received a telephone call that lit up my insides like the aurora borealis. North Star's previous owner rang me to ask if I would still like to take him back. With a smile as wide as the ocean, I beamed and immediately replied, 'Yes, yes I would very much like to have him back, one million percent, yes.'

It seems that North and I do indeed have a part two of our journey together. With indefatigable belief, I have patiently waited, endured the years of being horse-less once again, and deeply mourned the loss of my very own beloved North Star.

I can't help feeling that the timing is too beautiful and perfect as well. It feels like he is coming back to walk beside me during the next phase of my work and with the birthing of my first book. There are no words. It is simply perfect.

Appendices

Appendix 1

Alternatives to the Body Scan

At times and with certain clients, it will not be appropriate or necessary to do a full Body Scan, so employing some briefer techniques for connecting to the body can be really helpful and enables you to adopt a flexible approach with your clients to meet their needs on any given day.

Here are a few alternative ways for you and your clients to make a connection with the body. These exercises work better with the eyes closed but can be done with them open too.

Remember that in all this practice, we want to notice and witness what is happening in our body, ask our body for its guidance and wisdom and start to move through life from an embodied position. As with the full-length Body Scan, these techniques naturally bring about relaxation and grounding, but their main aim is to encourage us to listen to our body and start to encourage it to speak to us. Over time they bring about a mind-body connection and a greater sense of general well-being.

A Simple Mind-Body Connection:

- Sit or stand quietly, preferably eyes closed but this is not essential.
- Notice how your head feels.
- Notice how your breathing is.
- Place one hand on your heart and the other on your lower belly.
- Just feel your body for a few minutes.

- If appropriate, ask them if they have a noticeable sensation anywhere. Often people will be able to find something that they weren't aware of before starting the exercise. Ask them to describe it, letting them put their words, imagery and metaphors on it.
- Simply get them to focus on the sensation and then proceed to use this as a regular check-in point as the session proceeds, for example: 'How does that tightness in your belly feel now?' 'Has it come back?' 'Has it changed in any way?'

Breath-Focused Connection:

This exercise helps people learn to breathe correctly and to start to deepen their breathing, thus lowering arousal levels and facilitating a more present and grounded state, which is more conducive for equine work.

The correct way to breathe is for the chest and belly to rise outwards on the in-breath and to fall inwards on the out breath. Many of us breathe incorrectly until shown this so it can take some practice to become coordinated to begin with. Over time it will become more natural.

- Simply put your attention on your breathing just as it is.
- Don't try to change it, just notice the quality of your breathing.
- Is it shallow? Tight? Or deep and long?
- Are you breathing in the upper part of your chest only?
- Can you feel your breath in your belly too?
- Once you have a baseline reading, then consciously focus on changing your breathing.
- Placing one hand on your chest and one on your lower part of your belly, beneath the belly button, can be very helpful and comforting.

- Gently aim to take longer breaths, maybe counting to three on each inhale and exhale to begin with, then gradually building to four, then five and so on.
- If the breath is solely felt in the chest, encourage it to move gently down into the belly. Use imagery or metaphors that work for the client, for example, you might suggest that they imagine a balloon in their belly and try to inflate it gently a little more on each breath. Talk about their hand moving outwards on the inhale and moving inwards on the exhale.
- The aim is to try to shift the breath to being more in the lower belly than the chest. This aids relaxation and calmness, it is also grounding.
- After a while, ask the client again how the quality of their breathing is and how they feel now compared to when they first connected to their breath.
- Again, use this connection to their breathing throughout the session as a marker for how they are feeling and especially if the horse changes its response dramatically, as this can be an indication of tension in the client or they might be holding their breath.

Heart Focused Connection:

- Begin with some gentle breathing for a minute or two. Placing hands on the chest and belly can help.
- Then get the client to put their attention on the heart area. Placing both hands on the heart can help.
- Ask if they can feel their heartbeat. If they can't, get them to imagine that they can.
- Also ask them to get a general immediate sense of how their heart feels. Is it soft and open? Receptive and loving? Or is it closed? Tight? Contracted?

- What is the emotion they feel when connecting with their heart?
- Once they have their baseline, suggest that they visualize their own heart and again encourage imagination if necessary as not everyone is visual.
- Ask them what color it is.
- How big it feels.
- Any areas that feel darker or lighter, etc.
- Then simply ask them to ask their heart what it needs or would like from them in that moment. Or, if they have a decision to make, such as which horse to choose to work with, suggest they ask their heart for the answer.
- This technique can also be used in direct relation to a horse or a herd. The client can first connect with their heart and ask it what it would like. Then turn to face the horse/s and ask their heart again for further information, which horse to choose, or what they would like to experience with a particular horse on that day.

This simple technique is so effective and reliable it is astonishing that we agonize so much in life about which path to choose! It works every time and seems to provide much more reliable and congruent decisions for people. It is also, of course, a brilliant method for connecting to horses as they respond much more positively to us when we come from a heart-centered place.

Grounding Technique:

For clients who need to pull their energy down into their body if they have very active minds and the horses are not cooperating as a result, this can work well. By the way, it is also a technique that I highly recommended all equestrians use *before* riding.

- Get them to close their eyes and just notice where their breath is located in their body.
- Get them to scan all the way down their body briefly and notice where their breath seems to stop.
- This will tell you where there is a blockage. Often this is above the level of the pelvis but not always.
- Now use the breathing technique as described above but now also add the following:
- Suggest they imagine a funnel, tube or pipe in their abdomen, which goes out through their pelvic floor or base of their spine, down their legs and feet and into the ground.
- Imagine the pipe is clear and can carry their breath. That there is an easy flow to it and that it works almost like a pump or bellows.
- Then suggest that they imagine they are breathing down into this pipe and down into the earth. Keep emphasizing the word *down*, and focus on the pelvis, legs and feet as they begin, this encourages the breath and energy to move downwards.
- Keep this going for a few minutes or until you sense a change. If they are struggling remind them to breathe gently and imagine as much as they need to.
- If appropriate, you can suggest that on the out breath they send their breath down into the ground and as they inhale they draw clean, revitalizing earth-energy back up into their body.
- Check-in with them again to see where their breath is now located in their body.
- Has it shifted down past the block?
- If yes, then find out where it can now be felt. The aim is to be able to feel the breath moving freely down the legs and into the feet and ground.

- If it is blocked in another place, repeat the exercise and locate the pipe/tube at the new place, maybe going out from the legs or feet.

These are just a few additional ways to start making a connection to the body; there are many more possible variations. As with everything, practicing these regularly yourself first is the key to being able to safely and gently guide your clients through the new skill of connecting to their body in a positive and supportive way.

APPENDIX 2

Group Safety Agreement for Creating a Safe, Sacred Space

When in a group setting our aim is to hold the 'sacred space of possibility'* an engaged form of awareness which allows for all participants to each have their authentic experience and involves practicing the following:

1. Confidentiality: What is shared stays among this group.
2. Share from personal experience by using 'I' statements when giving feedback to others.
3. Look for the positive in each other and our sharing.
4. Release evaluation and judgment of self and others.
5. Uphold the principle of the 'Talking Stick' – when one person is talking everyone respects them and holds the space for them with positive regard and complete focus.
6. Tears are welcomed as a natural part of the process.
7. Ensure emotional safety by honoring all emotions as valuable sources of information and positively encouraging expression of emotions, even if uncomfortable.
8. Remember, emotions are contagious. With this in mind, it is better to take time to acknowledge and feel into your emotion or share it briefly with the group, e.g. 'I'm feeling nervous today' is sufficient without going into details and diffuses the energetic effect of suppressed emotions within a group.
9. Honor this space as a 'should' free zone (or our False Self voices).
10. Hold the 'sacred space of possibility'* for others to have their authentic experience both in the full group and during individual sessions.

11. Take care of our own needs and not try to meet others' needs, including the horses.
12. As the need arises, participants may leave the group and room for a quiet time of reflection or ask the facilitator for time to process with them.

Based on the group safety rules originally produced by Eponaquest® and modified by Angela Dunning.

*This phrase was coined by Kathleen Ingram, Co-Founder of the Eponaquest® Apprenticeship.

Appendix 3

The Eponaquest® Authentic Community Building Agreements

1. Maintain confidentiality.
2. Refrain from using others' vulnerabilities against them.
3. Use emotion as information, communicating the information behind the emotion to avoid shaming others in the name of 'authenticity'.
4. Sit in uncomfortable emotions without panicking, recognizing that emotions can be contagious.
5. Resist the temptation to 'fix' people, horses, and uncomfortable situations.
6. Read 'misbehavior' as a form of communication, recognizing the learning edge of others.
7. Demonstrate sensitivity, flexibility and responsiveness to personal space and boundaries, yours and those of others – people and horses.
8. Focus on the present. Notice which emotions belong to the current situation and which belong to the past, including projection and transference.
9. Pay attention to the dynamics of shared emotion, empathy and emotional resonance.
10. Distinguish between instructive personal feelings and conditioned (False Self) emotional patterns.
11. Create a psychological container of support, holding the 'sacred space of possibility'* as a fully engaged form of patience.
12. Activate the Authentic Self, thus enabling innovative solutions.

* This phrase was coined by Kathleen Ingram, Co-Founder of the Eponaquest® Apprenticeship.

Linda Kohanov is the author of this document and these agreements are based on a sequence that originally appeared in the book *Riding Between the Worlds*. [11/12]

APPENDIX 4

21-Step Checklist:
Honoring the Horse's True Role in Equine Facilitated Practice

1. The horse has clearly indicated that he/she is happy to undertake equine facilitated practice.
2. The horse is regarded as a sentient being in his/her own right.
3. You seek to provide a service in equal partnership with your horse, offering an inter-species modality for the benefit of your clients and enjoyment of your horses.
4. The horse has a choice about working or not on any particular day, and also which client/s or not to work with as far as possible.
5. The horse has a voice *and* it is listened to.
6. The horse is kept well, healthy and fit enough to do this work, otherwise he/she has time off.
7. The horse lives out in a herd with sufficient access to company, shelter, food and water.
8. The horse's lifestyle is balanced with regular breaks, time off and opportunities to engage in other activities that he/she enjoys.
9. You work towards removing all forms of control and dominance in your relationships with your horses, including techniques and equipment and in your relationship approach.
10. The horse's physical, emotional and spiritual boundaries are respected at all times.
11. You trust your horse to carry out his/her role and do not interfere with his/her suggestions, feedback or actions unless safety becomes the priority.
12. You pay attention to your horse's feedback at all times and

strive not to ignore or override this.

13. You carefully manage the ratio of number of people to each horse, to avoid overwhelming, pressuring or frightening the horse.

14. You manage your own boundaries and avoid projecting your needs onto the horse.

15. You turn your horse out as soon as the session with the client is finished.

16. You hold the 'sacred space of possibility' and teach all your group participants how to do this in order to ensure a calm, mindful environment for the horse to work in.

17. You adopt a flexible approach, non-reliant on agendas and you keep your False Self in check.

18. You are willing to be humble and defer to your equine partner's suggestions and lead.

19. You are connected to your body, emotions and energy at all times to ensure congruency when working with your horse and adopt a mindful approach.

20. Your work focuses on relationship with the horse at all times and this takes priority over task completion or outcomes and is not outweighed by benefits to clients.

21. You support your horse's well-being through a blend of veterinary care and holistic management using appropriate complementary therapies to maintain his/her health and balance.

REFERENCES

1. Rector, Barbara K, CEFIP-ED. *Put the Power of Horses to work for you. Enhance quality of life, improve communication skills and acquire nourishing vitality – Haciendas Equine,* 2.5.2015.

2. Hallberg, Leif. *Walking the way of the horse: Exploring the power of horse-human relationship.* New York: iUniverse, cited in Sarah Watson, (2015). *An interpretative phenomenological analysis of client's experience of equine facilitated psychotherapy in literature: An interpretative perspective.* (2008).

3. Eponaquest® *Best Practice Guidelines,* July 2015.

4. Strozzi, Ariana. *Horse Sense for the Leader Within.* AuthorHouse, 2004.

5. Strozzi, Ariana. *Horse Sense for the Leader Within.* AuthorHouse, 2004.

6. Oxford Dictionaries online.

7. Morris Berman cited in Marion Woodman and Elinor Dickson, *Dancing in the Flames: The Dark Goddess in the Transformation of Consciousness,* (Shambhala Publications Inc., 1996), p.210.

8. Strozzi, Ariana. *Horse Sense for the Leader Within.* AuthorHouse, 2004.

9. Kern-Godal A, Brenna I H, Kogstad N, Arnevick EA & Edle R (2016). *Contribution of the Patient-Horse Relationship to Substance Use Disorder.* Int J Qualitative Stud Health Well-being 2016, (11): 31636. http://www.ijqhw.net/index.php/qhw/article/view/31636

10. Gehrke, Ellen Kaye., PhD; Baldwin, Ann., PhD and Schiltz, Patric. M., PhD. *Heart Rate Variability in Horses Engaged in Equine assisted Activities.* Elsevier Inc., 2011 Published in

Journal of Equine Veterinary Science 31 (2):78-84.

11. Avera, Cryshtal. *Managing Stress in Therapy Horses. Equine Therapy Horse Standard of Care Research Project.* Published on www.soulseekerjourney.com, 2016

Quote from Marion Woodman at the beginning of Chapter 6 taken from the *Marion Woodman Foundation* website: https://mwoodmanfoundation.org

Quote at the beginning of Chapter 4 taken from Kohanov, L and McElroy, K. *Way of the Horse: Equine Archetypes for Self-Discovery.* New World Library, 2007.

Quote at the beginning of Part II inspired in part by the words of Ren Hurst in *Riding on the Power of Others: A Horsewoman's Path to Unconditional Love. Vegan Publishers™*, 2015

Made in the USA
Monee, IL
07 January 2020

19974704R00143